Sacred Union:
The Journey Home

by
Sri Ram Kaa and Kira Raa

TOSA Publishing
PO Box 457
Tijeras, NM 87059
505-286-9267
www.tosapublishing.com

Typesetter: **Barbara Kruger**
Cover Designer: **Toni O'Bryan**

ISBN 0-974-9872-2-4

Library of Congress Control Number 2003092180

Manufactured, typeset and printed in the United States of America

This Text is Volume One of The Self-Ascension Series

Other Revealing Books by Sri Ram Kaa & Kira Raa

2012: You Have a Choice!
Archangelic Answers and Practices for the Quantum Leap

2012 Atlantean Revelations:
Becoming a Mystic in a 9 to 5 World

Sacred Self-Ascension
Cards of Clarity™
*Your Journey of Insight, Discovery,
Wisdom & Remembrance*

On DVD:

Sacred Yoga for Everyone!
The Yoga of Self-Ascension

Soul Nourishment for
The Tentative Vegan

Available Through
TOSA Center for Enlightened Living
PO Box 457
Tijeras, NM 87059
Phone: 505-286-9267
www.selfascension.com

Living Self-Ascension,
A second edition sharing from Sri & Kira

Sacred Union shares the experiences and rapid transformation we experienced during the first six months of our reunion. Our relationship with the Divine, with the assistance of Archangel Zadkiel, opened portals of connectivity and wisdom that to this day are still bearing fruit. The realizations and the energies found their way into our core and have birthed a process of ever-refining authenticity. In short, the path deepens as does our love and gratitude.

Drawing upon the wisdom shared by Archangel Zadkiel and incorporating powerful self-healing practices, we have developed a home study program entitled: Navigating The Inner Matrix. This 9-week course has assisted thousands of people worldwide to find greater Peace and Freedom in their lives. It also prepares the student to anchor their Ascended Heart as the new foundation in their lives. Please visit www.SelfAscension.com to learn more.

Self-Ascension is a pathway to Source that is a resurrection of Spirit while still being in this world, having a body and a life to live here. For truth to become actualized it must be lived. We live the power and the healing of the Archangelic revelations and practices each and every day and enjoy true freedom. The Self-Ascended state is not only a pathway Home, it is also a path of connectivity that offers true Joy while living in the world.

We share more about this journey in our second book, "2012: You Have A Choice!" Each person must find their way. The sharings we offer in our writings are intended to awaken your own inner knowing. As we all learn to trust our hearts' wisdom more fully the world we share becomes more peaceful and nourishing for us all.

Many Blessings!

Sri Ram Kaa & Kira Raa

Advance Praise for
Sacred Union: The Journey Home

"Sacred Union is a divine blending of personal journey, love story and riveting spiritual teaching. The call to Transparency in relationship and the invitation to Authenticity are grounded in down-to-earth techniques. This is required reading for the new millennium!"

Melanie I Mulhall, Author
Living The Dream—
A Guidebook For Job Seekers And Career Explorers
Dragonheart and
Dragonheart Publishing, LLC

"Yes! Yes! Yes! Sacred Union: The Journey Home, is filled with powerful insights and Divine Wisdom. This is a life-changing book. . .I loved it!"

Tom LaRotonda, Partner
Core Matters, L.L.C

"A wonderful book of personal reflection, spiritual inquiry and meaningful answers to life's ordinary struggles!"

Meredith Young-Sowers D.Div., Author
Wisdom Bowls: overcoming fear and coming home
to your authentic self and
Angelic Messenger Cards

"The book is simply marvelous! It is filled with love and service. Reading Sacred Union: The Journey Home, I felt waves of warmth, joy, and recognition. Your book is another true "revelation." I honor you both for your courage, trust, and love, as well as your commitment to share your experiences."

Paul Bodor,
Project Management Consultant

What People Are Saying About the Writings of Sri Ram Kaa and Kira Raa:

"Offering global reassurance and changing the consciousness of the world."

~ **Newsweek Magazine**

"The authors are lighting the way for readers to make their own decisions with eyes wide open. Whatever your spiritual path, religion, or background, there is sure to be something in this book that you will recognize and connect with. Are you ready for a quantum leap?"

~**Bookreviews.com**

"The authors provide some simple practices that are multi-dimensional and can be understood and followed by people of all religions as we approach a great shift."

~**Awareness Magazine**

"Wisdom Teacher Sri Ram Kaa and Angelic Oracle Kira Raa leave no stone unturned with their latest publication. They cover every aspect of modern human existence including romance, life lessons and preparation for the current global shift. Their unique voice expands his or her concept of reality. In the end, the reader is gifted with a different perspective of our earth, the universe and our place within it all."

~**Vision Magazine**

TOSA Publishing
PO Box 457
Tijeras, NM 87059
www.tosapublishing.com

Sacred Union: The Journey Home
Foreword for the Second Edition

"Spirit all-ways seems to keep us all on a need to know basis!"
...Kira Raa

The joy of bringing forth a foreword for a second edition of a book that miraculously took form in the last 30 days of 2003 is great gift! At the time that we completed Sacred Union: The Journey Home, we had no idea that it would literally touch thousands of lives, circle the globe, be the basis for a life-changing home study program, (Navigating the Inner Matrix), and be so popular that we would sell out of all print copies. Imagine our surprise when "rare" first edition copies were popping up on Amazon for $99 each!

Shortly after our first release of this powerful book, we fondly recall overhearing someone share with another, "Oh, it's a great book, a quick read", only to have the one they were speaking with respond, "I thought so too, until I read it the second time! And now that I am reading it for the fifth time I think I finally really get it!" We smiled and felt the Archangelic realm smile too.

This dialogue was actually a foreshadowing of the Divine loving wisdom of the Archangelic realm, that guided every word, every chapter, of this extraordinary manuscript. As you move through the pages what you will recognize is a depth of love that allows you the momentum of assimilation of the material at exactly the pace you are ready and willing to receive.

The process of Self-Ascension is one that cannot be easily defined, and yet it is one that is easily experienced. Imagine your life without any self-doubt? From this space of recognition all of the answers you seek effortlessly reveal themselves. To fully embrace living your life on a daily basis in the energy of Self-Ascended Peace, Love and Joy transcends the limiting beliefs that are carried in our emotional bodies and reinforced by those who seek to control our lives.

You, beloved one are FREE. You are free to have an amazing life, and the fact that you chose to pick up this book and begin this journey is your verification that you have already made that choice! Welcome home to your freedom. We celebrate you.

As you journey through this book, do your best to smile often, relax any judgment about yourself and others, and open yourself to interaction with the Archangelic realm in a way that is loving, nourishing and stimulating. After all, you chose to be here, on this planet, right now...it is YOUR TIME to celebrate.

Many Blessings of Abundant Love
Sri Ram Kaa and Kira Raa

PS: If you, like thousands others, feel called to deepen the connection you uncover through reading this book, please go to our website and learn about Navigating the Inner Matrix. Let your heart lead the way! www.SelfAscension.com

Contents

This text is a way to say "I love you."
I have welcomed you home.
And because you have been away so long,
Is it a surprise you would forget your way back?
Is it a surprise you would lose your identity
with me?
Is it a surprise you would need some help?
I come back at this time, in this manner, to bring
everyone a road map!

Archangel Zadkiel

Introduction by Kira

This beautiful book is a love story. It is a universal love story, and every word of it is true! Every word, every event, every scenario, is nakedly revealed and relayed with loving, careful detail.

September 2002

"Are you journaling about this?" he asked after yet another breathless phone call.

"Not really," I answered, silently wondering why he had asked.

"Well, I think we should be!" he stated with a clarity and power that scared me while exciting every part of my being. I knew he was right, and I had no idea why.

Had it really only been two weeks since we first met online? Wasn't I preparing to marry someone else? Why was I suddenly so available to throw it all away for a potential relationship with someone I had yet to meet in person!

Trust! I heard from nowhere. Did that concept just come out of me?

Was I *really ready* to walk my walk, talk my talk, and live from my heart as I had so often challenged others to do?

Trust! I heard again.

I was inwardly laughing at the irony of the professional intuitive being asked to trust that which she was hearing. Every day I so easily provided the bridge for others. My intuition had been escalating rapidly and with staggering accuracy as was evidenced by the constant stream of referred clients, and the two-week waiting period for them to see me.

February 1999

Pregnant at 39 with my second daughter, and during my attunement to Reiki Mastership, I first experienced communication with the Archangels.

I was in a deep, silent meditation, searching for the connection, waiting for my Reiki Master to attune me. Loving warmth suddenly filled my entire body and I felt a presence of energy surround me. It was then that the Archangel Gabriel announced himself to me.

He flew to me, brilliant with light, surrounded by a golden aura, and simply said, "You are Shakira." Consumed by the energy of love, coupled with the spiritual ether of the class and the meditation, it seemed natural to accept this name and this visitation. It just felt as it should be.

It was still many minutes before my teacher initiated the attunement. I continued in silent meditation, embraced by this state of joy and bliss. Opening my eyes, I saw my Reiki master standing before me. She gazed at me, the beauty of the divine sparkling in her eyes, as she said, "Yes, it is time; no more hiding!"

We hugged deeply, tears streaming down both of our faces.

I KNEW.

It was another two years before I accepted this as true, before I legally changed my name to Shakira, and before I embraced the shift in my life that came with this acceptance, with this amazing surrender. Now, even that name seems foreign to me, as my true identity has been revealed.

As you read this story of two people who came together, who experienced pain, fear, love and trust, you will surely discover your own keys to self-ascension.

As I did.
> *As we did,*
>> *…and as we do!*

Sri Ram Kaa and I, prior to meeting, had experienced the drama, the pain, and the semiconscious state of *believing* we were open, emerging, and living in the moment.

We each had always just about been there, just about broken through, and yet, were always just short of the mark, and just shy of the knowing, just shy of having genuinely accepted our authenticity, our core essence, of really living our authenticity and our awareness from the deepest levels!

It is not my story. It is not his story. It is our story, and it is a true story, simply told as it has so lovingly unfolded. We were blessed with the guidance of an Archangel. We are all blessed with the guidance of angels if we choose to ask, trust and listen. We always receive answers, if we are willing to trust!

We were also blessed in the guidance of a new way of eating, and a new pattern of nourishing ourselves on many other levels. This was most challenging and eagerly ignored at first. Yet, as we have continued to release our egoic selves, it has now become a sincerely embraced and welcomed part of everyday life.

We were blessed with the gift of releasing time as a false god. That is, we stopped living by the clock and instead simply followed our natural rhythms. We have been gifted with the recognition of many other false gods, and with each release we are enjoying ever more freedom and joy.

We are honored that you have chosen to share this experience with us and that you have chosen to listen to your inner guidance, to your angel.

We are honored that you have chosen to *know*.

All of us, *all six billion on this planet,* are potential "walk-ins," beings that possess the amazing ability to *walk-in* to our authentic selves at any time we choose.

- ❤ Beings who are lovingly blessed, and provided with the gift of experiencing life on this planet to assist us with our own evolutionary expansion.

- ❤ Beings who are so nourished that we are given the ability to obtain anything necessary to accomplish our individual, and yet, collective, mission at any time!

We only need ask, to ask with love and gratitude from our authentic center within.

When we walk-in to our authenticity, miracles are no longer a surprise. If an Archangel appears to us, we *know* it is our birthright. It is no longer a miracle that all flows, that the pieces fit, for that is also our birthright.

Anyone and everyone who has embraced success by any measure of society, while providing the gift of service to humanity, has had to face a struggle, experience the ghost in the closet, the deep secret. This struggle is part of the gift that brings them back to the One that they are, the One that we are, the One that YOU are.

May you also know that it is, indeed, *your time.* May you know the love and the bliss of your connection with the divine. Allow the miracles of your authenticity to continually pour abundant joy out to you, effortlessly, brilliantly, lovingly.

It is your birthright, it is my birthright, and it is the birthright of all! You simply need to remember, to ask, and to know.

Self-Ascension Model

The following page displays the Self-Ascension Model. This simple model was given to us for the benefit of all, by Archangel Zadkiel. The outer terms represent the steps we walk on the path to the rediscovery of our authenticity. The steps are not fixed by a specific order, therefore you may enter the model at any point. They are:

- ❤ Surrender
- ❤ Release Judgment
- ❤ Unconditional Love
- ❤ Be In Union

The central star represents the balance and the integration of the masculine and the feminine within the self. The Path of Self-Ascension (located in the center of the star), includes the pivotal experiences we encounter as we move through the four steps. The Path of Self-Ascension is:

- ❤ Peace Knows God
- ❤ Love Connects with God
- ❤ Joy Embraces God

The sections of this book are each a step of the Self-Ascension Model. Within each section you will find the experience of the path of Peace, Love and Joy.

You decided to pick up this book because the Authenticity of who you are is already activated, already growing inside of you, and ready to blossom!

The Self-Ascension Model

Four Steps for the Journey Home

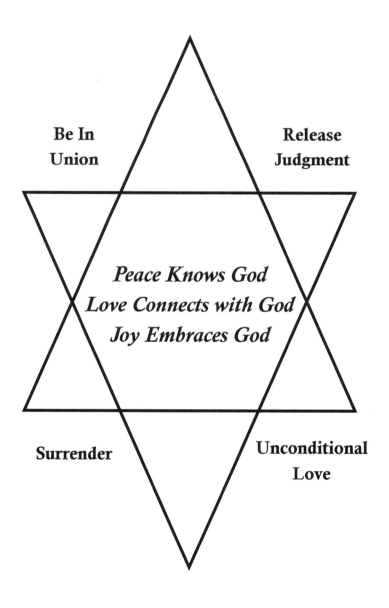

Be In
Union

Release
Judgment

Peace Knows God
Love Connects with God
Joy Embraces God

Surrender

Unconditional
Love

Section One
Surrender / Trust

As you awake
   Breathe
As you Breathe
   Give Thanks
As you Give Thanks
   Know that you are Love
As you are Love
   Know you are Light
As you are Light
   Know you are the Beacon
The Light
   The One
The Divine,
   who captured my heart

—*Kira Raa*

1

Shakira

December 31, 2001

My mind was racing again with the same self-bashing rhetoric …and it broke my heart as I felt the pain…*again!* Did I really just say that?

AGAIN?!

WHY was it *always* MY heart! What WAS wrong with me!…and just who, or what, is this god?…and just why WAS I here, on this planet, at this time?

After all, it was becoming harder to stay here, to hang out, to simply be! By all accepted standards I was certainly failing at life. I had been married four times, each one successively worse. Always entering the next marriage confident I had learned the lesson of release. The lesson that would prevent me from entering into yet another abusive relationship, only to have it return in a more painful experience. A repeating pattern that was consistently worse with each marriage!

I had lived through four abortions, enough said! *Or was it?* I had always been not white looking enough for the very white neighborhood in which I was raised. In the midst of the stereotypical perfect American neighborhood of athletic, thin, blonde, blue-eyed girls, I stood out as a thick-haired, brown-eyed, dark-skinned outcast. I had an ethnic last name, and preferred art and music. Basically, I had spent my entire life chronically unhappy with my curvy figure and appearance.

The reality that I was *different* was a bitter pill to swallow. I so wanted to just be normal, just fit in, yet that was an elusive fantasy. Having swallowed Hollywood's image of what a woman should be, why was it amazing to me that I couldn't understand my battle with depression?

Medicate vs. don't medicate. Love myself, sure, but how? Where WERE the answers? Based on my life experiences to date, I knew they could never be inside of *me*…could they? Yet, I was being called. There was a voice that was seeking to be heard, and it was providing me with new perspectives.

What if it had all been an illusion? What if I had truly just broken through? What if I finally understood all of the popular words and phrases? After all, I had read every book anyone ever suggested; that's where the answers were supposed to be, weren't they?

My ego answered for me. "Since you feel you have the answers and are still miserable, still seeking peace, then you are most definitely, certifiably insane!"

…And the loop started again, for if I was insane, there was only one answer: Medicate it! Quickly!

So I did! I medicated myself for two years, and happily gave myself to a medication-induced, dreamlike state of being. During this time I filed a **second** bankruptcy, and postponed confronting my darkest shadow. Yet I was unable to hold back what had to be, and so, without warning or preparation, I walked through hell itself.

January 1, 2002

Startling answers to my many questions began to surface. These answers, sought for years and so desperately needed, stirred my soul. I was aware of new feelings and perceptions, yet I was uncomfortable with them. I had not realized that so many of my questions were universal in nature, nor was I yet aware that the answers were universally available to all sincere seekers.

The most compelling vision of my life, granted to me on this first day of the New Year, occurred very early in the morning, around 3 a.m., as I lay alone in a warm tub filled with water.

I had struggled to climb the ladder of success one more time, simply to slip back down the lowest rung and lose it all *again*. I had already vacated my 6000-square-foot dream home in an elite mountain community near Denver, but I was drawn to spend this New Year's Eve back there. I slept on the floor of my former master suite, stared into the glowing fireplace, and realized I was leaving behind all I had considered important. Even more confirming of the failure was the complete awareness that *I* had created the environment for this lifelong struggle to culminate in the loss of everything the outside world of judgment (and I) considered important.

Still, I wanted to spend one last night in that opulent home. I wanted to take one more bath in an opulent tub, and make love one last time to the man who helped me realize that I was ready to finally put all abusive relationships out of my life, permanently.

Soaking in the tub, reviewing all that was wrong with my life, committing to the traditional resolutions of the coming year, and feeling like a 41-year-old failure, I sank into my opening.

A beam of golden white light appeared and started streaming toward my belly. It glowed around my entire navel, illuminating it, as I felt it enter me. I took note of the image of the beam around my navel as every cell of my body warmed and filled with love!

The love radiated up my spine and I felt it energize my heart, throat, and head. Then I felt it leave through the top of my head and stream back into the universe of love, connecting me to heaven, and revealing two totally different life paths that were open to me.

The first was the path of the known. I would always look much as I did then, never really happy with my body, yet able to tolerate it. I could stay with my current partner, and he would be loyal. I could even refinance my home and preserve the status quo. The familiarity and perceived safety offered by this path was initially comforting and attractive. I felt relief!

The second path was a complete surprise! I saw myself dancing. My hair was longer, there was a visible tattoo on my navel symbolizing this energy now entering me, and I was wearing a flowing cotton skirt and crop top. I lived in a warm climate, was married to someone I had not yet met, and experienced deep peace and happiness. I was encircled by others like this new me, loving, caring people that were free of self-loathing and filled with self-love. They wore contented smiles, and said, "Look how free she is."

I was immediately fascinated by this second path and surprisingly scared of it. I knew that choosing this path meant leaving behind everything I knew as true. I would be forced to trust forces over which I had no control, and I would forever be in service to the divine. Both of these paths revealed to me the choices I had available for completing my time on the planet.

Overwhelmed by actually seeing my options before me, like an abbreviated movie, the love and compassion for myself was completely all-encompassing. I instantly knew which path I wanted, the one I had been searching for all along. In the knowing, I simultaneously felt ecstasy and pain.

In the months prior to this moment, I had struggled to end yet another unhealthy relationship, and had been on my knees before God begging for answers. Now here I was, in a tub, in a vacant home that represented the completeness of my failure, and yet I was being given the gift of clarity, the certainty to move forward. I embraced gratitude.

My mind raced, processing a world of polarities I had never really understood until that moment. It was apparent I had enjoyed the drama of the polarities (love and pain, joy and sorrow, etc.). I embraced polarity, and actually had grown quite adept to the perception of flourishing in it!

Suddenly, absolutely, I KNEW it was all a GIFT! For 41 years I had been living in a waiting-for-the-other-shoe-to-drop reality of illusion, and all of it, the pain, the sorrow, the loss, everything was and IS a Gift!!

I was amazed that I already had the answers, *already knew* what I needed to know at the deepest essence of my core. It made me deeply sad. I was instantly aware of both the bliss and the abject fear of the knowing. (I refer to it as the knowing simply because it was deeper than acknowledgment and much closer to terror!) I was terrified my life would never be the same...*it hasn't been!* I was terrified of rejection...*I was rejected!* I was even terrified that I might finally have nothing to complain about! And in that moment of the recognition of my path, I found complete peace (even though I still struggled with this new insight for another year!).

I now knew what it felt like to truly touch God, to be clear, to be in the moment, to be complete with the Oneness.

This New Year's vision was the doorway into a series of miraculous events culminating with complete surrender on April 17, 2002.

After this vision and prior to April 17, my life was a whirlwind of activity. Taking care of my two daughters, struggling financially, ending the relationship with my partner, and walking through fear. My children were amazingly resilient and great teachers for me during this turbulent period.

Early in April, tragedy struck our family. Our beloved Shar-pei was in a freak accident that led to the painful decision to say good-bye to him. The pain was excruciating, and it was during his burial in a high-altitude aspen forest that another vision appeared to me.

The sun was glorious, the day was windy, but warm. As I looked up from a meditation I saw the love of God shining down on me. I clearly received the message, "You must go away for four days and four nights." It was also made clear to me that I was to fast, and observe silence during this time.

Go away! Who would take care of my children? How could I ever justify going away when money was so tight? Why was I going? I could not eat or speak? This was madness, again.

Yet, madness or not, I listened. When I finally allowed myself to peacefully consider the message during meditation, it was obvious, it was to be done. The preparations were made, and I left for the journey.

April 17, 2002

I knew that I was correct to follow this vision, even though my egoic mind was screaming at me to simply not go. There were many valid reasons why this was not the right time.

Yet, for the first time, I truly knew the deep meaning of trust. So I continued packing, made arrangements for my children, and left in the morning. Sunday afternoon, after a three and a half hour drive, I arrived at the rustic lodge where I would nest my simple belongings. Later, I treated myself to a therapeutic massage at sundown to symbolize relaxing into my body and into the silence.

The lodge provided a great source of love. An impromptu group New Agers in their forties, lovingly played guitar in the living room. I sat quietly nearby, meditated to the music, and then retired to bed trusting the process and eager for morning.

I awoke exhausted, unable to gain energy for anything. I could barely get out of bed. What was happening? I eventually forced myself to leave the room. I kept hearing a voice say *"there is not time,"* and removed my watch. I did not look at it again, nor have I worn one since.

Summoning what little energy I had, I sank into the hot springs on site. I wondered what was happening to me. The day was a blur.

Before retiring that evening I sank to my knees before the altar I had made in my room. Crying out in silence to God, I implored, "Why did you call me here? What am I doing? Why am I so unclear? Help me, I'm scared." I assured myself that I would awaken the next day energized, refreshed, prepared.

Tuesday, I awoke early and discovered that I felt much better. I began my day in meditation and then decided to go to the hot springs again for nourishment. Walking outside, I discovered spring snow, extreme cold, and the hot springs closed! Why was this happening? Why were all of my plans being thwarted? Had I made a mistake? How could my intuition be so off? Maybe a change of environment, so I left the lodge in search of something! I had no idea what. I was confused and still unclear. Why was I called here?

Praying ardently, I asked God what I had done, why was this state of confusion and disharmony happening? I could not stop the tears of sorrow and yet I could not find the reason for my tears either. Feelings of failure were large and lofty and my ego grabbed onto them with gusto, assuring me that if I simply talked and ate, all would be well. I chose to ignore my ego and to trust my higher guidance; but my ego demanded attention!

I wanted a break. I felt trapped within myself and I was feeling like I let myself down. I argued with myself that it was okay to go into town and order a latte. After all, that was like water, right? That wasn't food, was it? My ego was amazingly adept at offering me this foolhardy advice, so I surrendered and ordered the double tall vanilla soy latte. In a complete state of confusion, I was totally unable to focus. Feeling compelled to read and to write, I found the town park, but only after I found the mini-mart and an ice cream sandwich! My latte needed balance. Right? Old habits were intruding on the space I had cleared for communion, and I wasn't doing much to stop them.

The writing I did at the park was clearing and illuminating. It led me to a deeply needed recognition and set the stage for what was to come. Complete with my adventure in town, I finally made it back to the lodge for the evening. I was now clear that it was only myself that was holding me back from the accomplishment of this mission. It was time to enter the now re-opened hot springs once again, to cleanse my illusionary mind, and to prepare.

Yet, nothing! I sat in bed and vacillated about staying. Should I leave? Was this futile? What had I accomplished? I felt like a failure and went to sleep crying out to God, again. I was messing up my own vision quest!

Overwhelming sadness engulfed me as I awoke Wednesday morning. It arrived with its good friends, remorse, guilt, and indulgence. I was ashamed, feeling like an ungrateful devotee at the feet of the Master.

I had but one choice: get up, get out, and make the most of this day. God had called me here and it was important for me to honor that. I asked to be given guidance and opened one of the little meditation books that were on my altar and the phrases that appeared before me were perfect. The words were filled with reassurance, love and divine compassion. I no longer felt the shame or guilt, only the love of the Divine.

It was a sign! Thank you, God! I was complete. Offering my humble thanks to all the saints, angels and God, I went into a deep meditation, no longer feeling embarrassed in the midst of my connection with the cosmic consciousness. Instantaneously, I was told that I must stay, that I was ready, and that *today* was the day of clarity. With renewed faith and energy, I quickly left for the nearby National Forest.

I knew my destination. I had passed it before and had felt it call to me, yet I had not trusted myself enough to stop and explore. After three days of spring weather in the Rockies, the wind had finally calmed down. This break in the wind provided me the opportunity to safely traverse the steep grade down to arrive at this magical spot. Grateful that I had received good mountain training the previous summer, I made it to the bottom with little struggle. I stood at the edge of a magnificent and powerful river. The flow was swift and the rushing water was both clear and extremely cold. It was alive with fragrant, abundant nature on both shores.

Scanning the shores for my spot, I quickly discovered a large flat stone. Right in the middle of the river, it was not too far from where I stood. I determined that I would be able to make it to the stone from the shore. Taking a deep breath, I proceeded to gingerly find my footing on substantially smaller stones until I was in the middle of the river and standing on the large stone. Once there, I found the stone to be luminous, flat, and representative of the infinite. Unaware of the strength of this ageless wonder, I took my wool blanket, folded it into quarters, and assumed a meditative posture on the stone.

It was glorious: the warmth of the sun, the sound of the water, the energy of the lush forest, *the love!* I was overwhelmed by a loving God who was providing me with so many incredible gifts, and who was doing so with immense kindness in the face of my many transgressions!

In the fullness of this experience, I felt compelled to open my eyes. Spying at me from across the river was a graceful and perfect aspen staff, standing like Excalibur. It was calling to me, perched perfectly and waiting for me to claim it from the opposite shore. Standing to go forth and make my claim, I became aware that navigating toward my newly found Excalibur would be much more difficult than I initially perceived.

For some time, I stood on my stone, trying to decide which way to go, searching for the simplest path. I kept reassuring myself with the fact that the worst thing that could happen was that I would get wet. I felt that the retrieval of the staff, of my Excalibur, was being given to me as a test of faith. After all, didn't God always test?

I chose my route and started my pursuit of the holy Excalibur. I would pass this test. With each step, I felt closer to my goal. Then, about 1/3 of the way toward my holy Excalibur, I had the sudden realization that there was a simpler way to cross the river and it was okay to take that path. Keeping my precious Excalibur in my sight, I backtracked to the simpler crossing point.

As I approached the easier route, I found myself surrounded by magnificent old growth aspen. Each towering tree offered wisdom and support. Drawn by their energy, I did not notice the ground below and tripped over something in the tall grass. I looked down to see a seasoned staff of Aspen at my feet and felt the energy of its love reach up to engulf me.

Bending down to touch this magnificent staff, my eyes gazed across the river to my beloved Excalibur. From the perspective of clear eyes filled with love, it no longer appeared perfect. It was gnarled and dangerous, for in my hand was *my Excalibur,* along with the great gifts of perspective and discernment.

I sank to my knees in gratitude. I cried with recognition. I arose with Excalibur in my hands, and I knew! God did not intend for it to be so hard! I did not have to pass any test, except the test of whether or not I could trust myself.

I gave thanks to the staff across the river for calling me, for providing me with the opening to the path, for leading me to the ancient one. As I stood there, motionless, I felt a native chant enter me. I sang it strongly and out loud, dancing a native dance while giving thanks and praise to the planet. The need to commune with this fragrant gift of the earth was overwhelming and comforting.

Searching for a thorn, I found a berry bush, and pricked my finger on the thorn of one of its branches. I mixed my blood with berry blood. Through this impromptu ritual, I offered my love to God, to the planet, and to all of its inhabitants. I surrendered completely to the will of God. I accepted the task of sacred completion of my mission for this lifetime. Not knowing what I was truly surrendering to, I simply embraced and accepted the love of God; that was amazingly enough!

The stone was now beckoning me to return. With Excalibur firmly in hand, I turned and started my way back. Making my journey down the shore of the river, the sprouted grass called to me. As wheat symbolizes growth, I asked the grass if it wanted to join me. Three stalks leapt into my hands. A few more steps and a branch of aspen offered itself to me from the floor of the forest. I honored its request, joining it with my bouquet of grass.

Filled with the empowering flow of the earth, love of the planet, and the magic of the Divine, I laid Excalibur on the ground by the river's edge. It felt as if the branch itself had asked me to do this prior to returning to my stone. I humbly honored this request. Across the heavenly aspen altar I laid the grasses and the smaller gentle aspen branch. I prayed. I felt protected, safe. I turned and gazed into the river, then looked up at the sky, my head held upward, my arms outstretched. Embracing joy and love, repeating the same native chant over and over again; twirling and swirling...I was one with devotion and joy!

Stirring back to consciousness in the cold river, I realized that I was covered in mud and rocks. Up to my waist in freezing cold water, still spinning internally, it felt as if a force greater than myself was picking me up. It spoke, "come now, sit on the rock, and meditate in the warmth of the sun."

I do not remember pulling myself onto the rock. I do not remember being in the river. I do not know how long I was there before *the voice* pulled me out. Somehow, I was back on the rock, centered, and in a meditative posture, still begging God to speak with me directly and begging to know how I could serve. Deeply grateful, I thanked God for this day, this moment, this life, this magnificent planet.

More native chanting came from my heart and I savored the sun. *It was then the miracle happened.* I started to see the gold again and it was similar to the gold that had appeared to me on January 1st. The golden white light appeared to me now as a star. My hands rose to honor it and as they did, the light transformed into a pyramid. It was glowing, vibrant, and directly in front of me.

Everything in my view melted. For a moment, I felt as if I was in ancient Egypt. My hands came to be one over the other, palms up, over my third eye, the sixth chakra. Then they spread, forming a circle, gathering energy as they came to rest over my heart.

The need to return to the present was overwhelming and I allowed my eyes to again take in my surroundings. Across the river, on the opposite shore, stood a proud and tall Native American in full ceremonial dress. He was draped in turquoise and appeared to be a warrior. Asking for his blessing, I felt worthy, yet unsure. Was I ready? I asked to be gifted with his warrior power and I asked for protection. He was strikingly beautiful, powerful, and strong in his presence.

He answered my prayer. Moments later, a male African lion appeared next to him. I gasped in fear, then felt myself opening to the spiritual vision. The eyes of the lion stared directly into mine. We were locked in communication. I welcomed him to move forward, yet he simply stood, shared great love and wisdom with me and stated: "I am your totem."

Feeling the need to clear my eyes and begging to stay focused on the glory of God, my mind was wandering. Should I write this down? Will I forget? The answer came in the form of an inner thought: *How can you ever forget that which has always been?*

My mind wandered and I wondered if others would think I was crazy or simply fabricating a story. An answer came again: *"Learn to bring a recorder, learn the chants; you may bring another to do the recording of your conversations only if their heart is truly pure."*

Conversations! What conversations, and why would I need a recorder? I had no idea then what was ahead, and how prophetic this experience was!

Trying to stand I shivered, chilled to the bone. I must have been in the icy mountain water for a long time. My cotton clothes were sopping wet. Unable to stop my teeth from chattering, I looked at my hands. They were blue. I needed warmth. The hill that I needed to climb to return to my car seemed ominous and challenging. I was frightened.

Navigating back to the shore from my stone, I stopped to give thanks to this magical place. I bent down to pick up the aspen, the grasses. Do I take the Ancient One? *Yes,* I think to myself and grab it firmly. After only three steps, I clearly heard that the Ancient One was to stay. The new branch was to come with me. It was sad yet comforting to surrender my Excalibur back to the forest and to proudly walk back into the world with my new Excalibur. I was ready to serve, ready to share, ready to experience love and oneness.

My heart was pounding as I tried to climb the hill, my breath heavy and labored. Somehow, I was able to drag my half-frozen body back to my car. As I arrived at the car, it was now quite apparent that I was indeed suffering from hypothermia. I needed to remove my clothes. I started the car, turned on the heater, and remembered I had no other clothes with me, only a wonderful scarf.

My friend Thia, had insisted I have lodging for the trip and offered to me a beautiful scarf to accompany me on my journey. Until that very moment I did not know why the black velvet scarf had come with me on this journey. Now it became my savior.

Silently blessing my dear friend for the gift, I wrapped myself in the fringed scarf with the rhinestone-studded lotus. As I was warming in the car, I succumbed to great laughter at the abundant joy of the universe. I screamed out loud that I finally understood the benefit of humor and the gift of gratitude. I felt absolutely perfect wearing only my scarf, wrapped in love, joy and peace.

I intended to immediately start writing to God about this amazing experience of love when it was God who was speaking to me… hurry…get back…now is the time! I felt urgency as I raced back to the lodge. Pulling into the parking area, reality set in. I would have to walk in wearing nothing but a scarf! Perfect. Let all conventions, all illusions drop. I laughed to myself at the irony of this moment. Like a newborn babe I released any remaining modesty and jumped out of my car. I proudly walked through the lodge in my black velvet scarf, and went to my room to begin writing.

Settling into warm, dry clothes, the sound of drums called to me from below. Knowing it was important to be in the energy of the drums, I collected my journal, walked downstairs, and settled onto a very old comfortable couch. The combination of the drums and the cozy couch emanated an energy that was amazingly nourishing.

The spectacular gift of being in the presence of these free spirits who drummed passionately moved me to adopt a meditative posture on the couch. Over an hour later I awoke to find them still drumming, still loving. They had been lovingly supportive of yet another experience that appeared for me on this miraculous adventure.

Rested and nourished by the energy of the drumming, I heard the call of the wilderness again. I listened. Not knowing my destination, I allowed my energy to follow the call, jumped into my car and allowed the love vibration to guide me. Higher and higher into the wilderness I was called, until the road would go no further.

I got out of my car, found myself chanting and singing, twirling and swirling, and when it was over, I clearly heard: *You now walk between two worlds and you will do so from now on.* I had finally come home; I was freed from the illusion! The world of appearances no long held me in its grip. I was frightened beyond belief but knew that I could not, no, I would not, ever be able to step back into my old life.

Many events have happened since the time of that wondrous encounter. What had been my life was steadily and rapidly peeling away. I disbanded my business, despite my nagging fear of how I would support myself and my two children. I found the courage to say goodbye to my treasured personal assistant, who had been the closest thing to a real friend I had ever known. I filed bankruptcy and lost my home and brand new Lexus.

I began trusting myself enough to give intuitive readings for a living. I even relaxed into spiritual communication without fear. With the loving help and moral support of a new friend, I continued to grow. Clients found my intuitive advice to be loving, nourishing and helpful. I was ever more grateful for the guidance that was now consistently present in my life.

Not many months later I faced my biggest challenge to date. My two amazing daughters left their home with me to live with my older daughter's father and his new family. This was an unexpected and heart-searing event. I had spent every day of their lives with them! Yet my older daughter needed reconnection with her father. It had been twelve years since she had any contact with him, and she often suffered with numerous unexplainable illnesses. My heart knew she needed to heal and that my love for her was not enough. My three year old simply wanted to be with her sister and her daddy. I knew separating them was not an option. So, again, my ego was tested, along with my commitment to the Divine pathway.

Acutely aware that my older daughter needed to be with her father, I summoned all of my courage and called my ex-husband. He was lovingly responsive. Within 48 hours of that call, the chain of events that would lead to their moving in with him and his new family were in place. It was painful, yet I knew it was right for all of us. This, too, had been divinely guided.

The wave of loss I experienced was enormous. Daily I would become stunned and overwhelmed at how much I was being asked to release. Even my expensive clothing and accessories were given away so that I could embrace a simpler life. Often I felt enormous pain. Somehow, through it all, I was remarkably able to stay present with the abundant gifts of love, joy, remembrance, and gratitude.

I was embroiled in another challenging love relationship. My dearest friends were too dismayed by the events in my life and eventually left. My mother worried and my brothers were convinced that I was crazy. Finally, after the release, the pain, the surrender to the Divine, arrived the greatest gift of all…the oneness.

September 13, 2002

"Escalator to Expansion," read the subject line on his e-mail.

What was I doing even reading it, much less considering responding to it? Was I even still listed on that web service for spiritual singles? My current lover was in an ashram in India. My readings were going so well. I was a popular and very busy psychic in the best part of Denver. Why would I even begin to add more drama to my life by opening an email from a singles service?

Yet open it I did. I KNEW his energy. I KNEW he was the one. I KNEW we were destined to be together. I KNEW it was perfect.

Escalator to Expansion, indeed, I wrote back as my response. And so began my true mission on this planet. I finally accepted the greatest gift that was to be given to me at this time, the return to oneness with my soul partner, my masculine embodiment, a man named Jere.

As our mission quickly began to unfold, it all became clear. The puzzle pieces were finally all fitting together effortlessly. I understood the great release. I knew why the events of my life unfolded as they had. Jere was yet another miracle.

My mind raced and challenged me again. *You are risking everything…again!* Yet I knew it was time to move forward. It would be forever impossible to hide in the shadow. I was ardently aware that there was no one and no thing to rely on. Why would I do this to myself, why would I risk this…*again?* Yet, was this the same type of risk? There was a difference.

The answer that so eloquently revealed itself to me later appeared in an e-mail from Jere, himself.

For you see,
I am You
And
You, my love
Are me.

I knew then that the love of Jere and my trust in the universe were now united as the one. I knew that a flow of divine love was always available when there is complete trust. The only challenge left was to get out of my own way!

This acknowledgment and acceptance initiated my plunge into the deep well of authenticity, and I willingly dove in without further hesitation! I had no idea if anything or anyone would catch me. I was terrified, yet unable to stop myself. My trust in the Universe was complete and all-encompassing. Was this the leap into the arms of my Beloved, into the arms of God, into the authenticity of myself? Ready or not, I was about to find out.

*The second birth
Began with a whimper
No proud parents to wipe him dry
And hold him close.*

*Yet the entire company
Of heaven
Rejoiced.*

Sri Ram Kaa

2

Jerrold

January 2001

I was lucky. The woman I was divorcing honored that I was searching for something she could not provide. However, even with this knowing, ending an 18-year marriage was deeply painful. Divorce is heartbreak.

Even the most incompatible couples experience grief and a sense of loss when the status quo is upset. We are creatures of habit and find great safety in a predictable environment, even if the predictability is pain! As a relationship ends, we are cast into a sea of chaos upon which float islands of hope, freedom and excitement, and along whose shores are reefs of pain and grief. Such are the emotional waters that must be navigated on the way to creating a new life. And yet, with trust, patience and courage, there is an opening that always comes with the ending.

Guidance shows up in our lives in many amazing ways. It comes from the mouth of a stranger or from the loving perspective of a caring friend. Sometimes guidance comes in a more ferocious form, such as illness, job loss or other events that seem unkind or overwhelming. I have seen the hand of Spirit at work in my affairs and many others. In the long run we all seem to attract the experiences that we need to grow.

I was lucky. I had practiced listening to my guidance through meditation, journaling and paying attention to my own energy. I had always sought to understand the deepest mysteries, to look beneath the surface. This curiosity, coupled with a deep desire to serve, brought me into the field of psychotherapy during mid-life. My natural instincts to dive deep led me on a great adventure. I studied and acquired degrees in everything from conventional therapy to hypnosis, energy work and the newly emerging field of medical intuition.

I sincerely enjoyed assisting others with their personal challenges. Yet, there was always the feeling of something more that I was to be doing. I was painfully restless in my marriage and could no longer cultivate fantasies of a more fulfilling future with my current wife. I criticized myself for not working harder to enliven my marriage. *Take one more marriage workshop together, continue couples therapy…work harder at the relationship.* My inner self-talk was oriented toward improving the status quo and reinforcing my ego.

I never thought of myself as a prototypical New Age man, for I had been a successful businessman, private pilot, scuba diver, world traveler and…after all, I ate meat! Yet, I loved metaphysical workshops and was often one of the few male specimens in attendance. I had, step by step, progressed into an orientation toward the world that could only be called mystical.

My dear wife had stood by me during the stress-filled years when I was a stereotypical businessman. She stood by me during the bankruptcy. She worked full time while I went to graduate school to become a therapist. And she was still committed, even in the face of my inner turmoil, to stand by while I left the marriage. Although I admired her and was humbled by her commitment, I knew that the yearning I felt for expression and connection would not ever be fulfilled inside this marriage.

Let your soul lead. Let Spirit lead you to your highest expression. These were the principles that guided me. Often I interrupted the inner guidance by slipping into old addictive patterns instead of confronting my truth. The clues that the marriage was over had been present for years, yet we had always managed to cope. But each time I really looked, I had to acknowledge that I was not thriving, and neither was she. We were educated and had two bright loving children. We had a waterfront home, friends and financial security. We had completed lots of couples counseling, and had developed enviable communications skills, yet we were unable to create an environment where we both could thrive. Finally, I ended the procrastination and, mercifully for us both, I left.

It was an outrageous choice and it was a confusing choice. My inner voice screamed. I still loved my wife! I feared hurting her. I feared the judgment of others. I feared making a mistake to leave such a well-grounded woman. When I left I did not really know if it was forever, or just a period of personal renewal. I did know that to find the self in me that was longing for something more, I would have to cut the cords to the past. I needed to set myself adrift.

This was no mid-life crisis. I had experienced that adventure eight years earlier. This was a plunge into Trust. I had no idea where I was going or what I was to do. I only knew that I needed to be alone, really alone, and seek the spiritual clarity that would guide my next step. I knew that my soul was urging me onto my authentic path. First, though, I would have to transit the desert of the unknown, alone, without any plan. I had to leap off the solid ground of the predictable world and allow my soul to lead.

July 2002

It was now eighteen months later. I had sailed alone up the Inside Passage, camped in the Arizona desert, fallen in love in New England, and lived alone in Tucson. There had been the mystical visit to Peru, and the filling of countless journals with perceptions, fears, poems and musings. This journey had shaped itself for me, and now I found myself in San Diego.

Those past eighteen months had been a period rich with expansion through experience, personal growth, and spiritual Grace. Being free of career and family was a gift, leaving me with the opportunity to peel back layer after layer of emotional debris. I had cultivated a level of perception and trust that most men in our culture rarely experience. I found humility and I found my sacred heart.

My body hangs
like a mobile
on a windless day.

Suspended in the twilight
Between being and doing,
All the while
wanting neither.

And I notice
the passion I had felt,
the longing to be with You,
has transformed
into a peaceful knowing:
I AM You.

⁘

By the accepted standards of modern society, I was living on the edge of normalcy. I surrendered to whatever I felt called to, and learned that I could completely trust my soul. I progressed into an orientation toward the world that was poetic and mystical. I experienced exquisite beauty in nature, found deep peace sitting on rocks, and practiced meditation while waiting in bank lines! I laughed out loud at what most would consider inappropriate times, and openly cried at movies. It became my personal ministry to bring joy to people in supermarkets by offering humor and occasionally singing while riding the shopping cart at illegal speeds.

For the first time in my life I experienced spontaneous joy. It *was* simple. To experience joy one must love oneself and follow the flow of one's inner guidance. God does not expect us to live up to an artificial standard. God only expects us to be Authentic. I had learned through this time that listening deeply and trusting our inner guidance is, in fact, the highest form of morality. The rules that guided our behavior at age two simply do not apply at age twenty…we grow and evolve.

How will you ever know what is *truly appropriate* for you if you do not cultivate your inner listening? We hide our true feelings first from our parents, then from our friends, and finally from ourselves. In those months of living alone I discovered how pervasive my own self-deception truly was. I wanted a life without fear, a seemingly endless task. I had learned to step through my fears, yet fears still arose from time to time despite my feeling downright happy with my life and very connected to God.

I was feeling the joy of living a congruent life. My inner and outer beings reflected the same feelings, and I expressed my natural creativity, yet *there was still one missing element*. One day I found myself looking at the personal ad listings for an online singles service and chuckling to myself at the idea that I could find a compatible female online. Why not? Yet I was not looking for just a date; I wanted depth. How would I find someone who is truly congruent with my energy, my soul, based upon these listings?

I did not realize then that I had initiated the quest to find my soul mate. I was not looking for commitment. However, the depth of compatibility I expected was but a dream for many singles, including myself. I had stopped using the phrase soul mate because I believed that there were many compatible souls for each person on the planet. I was simply looking for depth and congruence.

Having put forth the intention to find an appropriate partner, I then proceeded to learn discernment by making mistakes! Fortunately, I was able to recognize that when a choice was not healthy, I could simply say *thank you* and make a new choice.

I had worked hard to develop an intuitive filtering method[1] that helped me immediately know whether a person's energy was compatible with mine. This technology motivated me to contact some very interesting people, people who were living life from a deeper place. Had I not pursued my own inner work I never would have recognized my Beloved Shakira. Meeting her was a fluke.

One evening, on yet another singles site, I placed my online search parameters in the system, hit search, and the screen announced that I had over 200 matches! Wow! Accidentally, I had searched nationwide instead of limiting my search to San Diego. Just as I was about to erase those hits and narrow my search to the San Diego area, an inner energy captivated my attention, and a new thought entered my mind: *There's someone for you in this list,* I heard distinctly and with power. This wasn't the voice of wishful thinking; it was the voice of guidance.

How many times in life had I heard that quiet dismissible voice inside? How many times had I really listened to it? The hunches that come from that voice offer rich rewards, and this time I listened!

First, I did this intuitive scan[2] without reading the text or consciously looking at the photos. I quickly scanned the pages of listings until I found the listing that tested[3] strong. Yes, there was one, a woman in Denver, Colorado, that was for me. I looked at her picture...there was something here. But what? Was there really

---

[1] In the field of Applied Kinesiology muscles are tested to diagnose true and false statements.
[2] See Note #1
[3] Based upon the use of Kinesiology

anything? Her biographical information did not really appeal to me, and there were no bells or angelic trumpets sounding off. There was simply a quiet voice inside that lovingly said *write her.* There was also another voice alongside that screamed *Denver is too far away; it's a recipe for heartbreak…she's not your type, she's tall with black hair and seems way too assertive!*

A few minutes later I went back and re-read the Denver woman's listing. There was a fuzzy recognition. *Contact her,* encouraged the voice. I felt vulnerable, yet I knew that I wanted to discover our soul connection, so I penned the first email. That first communication set off a chain of events that instantly transformed me and became the focal point of my life. Within 24 hours I was in love.

This was not the typical goo-goo-eyed, romantic cloud nine sort of affair. Instead, there was the excitement of recognition, the promise of union, the acknowledgment of Spirit, the expansion into a greater ground of being. When I talked with Shakira I knew that I had found the one who would complete me.

During the course of our email exchanges, we unwrapped a level of recognition that was stunning and, at times, frightening. When Shakira and I talked on the phone, the conversation would "time warp" and consume hours. Our breath would unite in passionate recognition, and our energy fields would combine, doubling in size. Even when we were not in direct communication I would feel her throughout the day, the energy between us further inspiring me.

❦

I felt you
this afternoon.
You silently draped your presence
on my heart
like an altar cloth.
Soothing, tender and sensuous
softly unfolding my resistance
—a sacred surrender—
and we blended;
a sacrament to love,
God's ultimate joy.

Precious passion!
Inspired through recognition;
Together we offer
The innocent prayer.
Love loving love
The Beloved loving the Beloved;
There is no higher kingdom.

We made the commitment to meet in person, and chose Sedona. The Mystical Mecca was to be our meeting place, for we both enjoyed the beauty of the red rocks and the serenity of the desert. Neither of us knew then that Sedona would spark an awakening that could be called mythical.

During the three weeks prior to meeting face-to-face, Shakira and I uncovered many similarities in our life paths. While the experiences of a man are different than those of a woman, the lessons we were working through in this lifetime were remarkably similar, including the methods we used for learning. We had both sought power in the world through business success. We had both lost that success through bankruptcy. We had both moved into the healing arts. More importantly, we were both completely aligned in our devotion to God. Through that alignment we experienced a trust in each other that dissolved any withholds.

We shared everything honestly, nakedly, and without holding back. As we shared everything without reservation, we cultivated a beautiful intimacy. This commitment is not just allocated to the past. Its power was in sharing what is alive in the moment and being transparent to each other through disclosure of thoughts, feelings and needs. By the time we met in Sedona, without being conscious of it, we had already begun the practice of Transparent Communication.

It was the Soul that had led Shakira and I to find each other. It was the Soul that initially dissolved the barriers to intimacy, offered forth conscious recognition of our connection, and provided the impetus for us to risk flying to another State to meet in person for the first time.

As the time to meet drew near, my ego was triggered by this relationship. Perhaps sensing the power of the upcoming Union, my personality-self flared with great gusto the day after I met Shakira in person.

October, 2002

From my journal: So intense these times! Last night and this morning I was knee deep in my stuff again. I felt my passion for Shakira melt in the face of my desire for a thinner, more Barbie-like girlfriend. It's hard to admit that I get turned on by the slender, supple feminine. And I feel terrible, criticizing myself for still holding this superficial standard for love. Ouch! My ego isn't getting what it wants. And I'm not enjoying any peace of mind. I feel tormented and torn inside.

I know that I am connected to Shakira in the deepest possible way. I know that we share a great potential together, that deep alignment and joy await me. I have seen the soul expansion. I have seen how similar we are. I have felt the deep peace, the thrill of finding my energetic match, the excitement of knowing that something grand awaits us. All the intuitive indicators have given thumbs up, green light, to this relationship.

And then I feel the anger rise up inside. I am pissed that she's not perfect. I am mad at God. Why haven't you given me someone with perfect teeth, smaller hips and maybe just a little less power. She can be intimidating at times!

And then I realized that my ego was looking for a girl, not a woman. I was looking to enjoy feminine energy without any risk of confrontation. I wanted someone who was weaker than I. Damn! I hated myself in that moment.

Then I wrestled with self-judgment: *You're shallow,* the inner voice condemned me. Shakira is an answered prayer: I feel grateful for her intelligence, her sensitivity, her wisdom, her intuitive abilities, her commitment to God, her artistic expressions. I value her ability to be candid and free, to be outrageous, to dance, sing and trust.

And yet in spite of these truths, in her presence I projected distance, fear and judgment. Then I would feel shame that I am superficial and less evolved than I thought. How do you spell torment? Self-judgment is hell. The beautiful learning was still ahead.

Dropping my judgment of her meant that I had to first embrace a deeper sense of self. A deeper love of me, to be at peace with my own body image, my own strength in the face of confrontation, my own self-worth.

At first I tried to reason with my ego. I would list on paper all the positive qualities I saw in my Beloved. Then I would list the shortcomings; it was a much shorter list. *There,* I proclaimed, as if making a sales presentation to a corporation, *the benefits clearly outweigh the shortfalls.*

This technique does not and did not work. I also do not recommend that you take a rational approach with the ego. Why? Well, as I experienced, to even try and convince your ego to change is absurd. The ego is your servant, not your equal, I kept reminding myself. And, more importantly, the problem is always one of self-love. All judgment toward others is a rejection of some part of ourselves. I realized that I could choose judgment or love.

Crying buckets of tears one morning, I was able to release the ego's grip and feel my love and my connection to Shakira again. I realized that in all my personal work, I had not tackled the relationship issue because I was not *in* a relationship. It was now time to dance with my dragons once again.

Spirit had brought to me my perfect mate. In the perfection of my relationship with Shakira, I had stimulated my own shadow. It was the relationship that brought to the foreground those areas where I was not fully accepting myself.

While this is normal in spiritually-based relationships, I had never before experienced it. Our partner will mirror our unfinished business, and it happened very quickly for me. Far more quickly than normal, and we did not even get an ignorance-is-bliss honeymoon! I found myself grateful and humbled for the lesson. The doors of my heart opened again and we explored Arizona together.

You are my Source
And my Destiny

You are the One
From which I came
And the One
I never left

Like a dog
Chasing its tail,
I know that what I seek
Has already found me.

Darling, do you really have the patience
To watch the annihilation of my ego?

Will you sustain Presence
In the face of its
dirty tricks,
heartbreak and despair?

Can you accept
That my efforts
To love your soul,
Worship your body,
And be present
with your personality,
will fall short
of your true value?

Sri Ram Kaa

3

Sri Ram Kaa Kira Raa

The Visions Begin; Jere Explains:

During our first outing in Sedona as I was driving in the Boynton canyon area Shakira suddenly lifted her hand and pointed.

"Pull in there," she commanded, pointing to a rough road on the right. "We're being called toward those mountains."

As I stopped the car at the end of the turnoff I objected. "Those mountains are miles away, let's drive closer."

"No, there's a path," she said, a mystical smile on her face.

I simply trusted, stopped the car, grabbed a water bottle and we began walking. She seemed to be pulled by an invisible tractor beam. I tagged along as the path disappeared. I was thinking it might be wise to drop some bread crumbs in order to find our way back.

She pointed to a dry creek bed in the parched desert floor. "Do you hear it?" She asked. We sat on the ground by a desert wash and quieted ourselves. I did hear a high frequency sound coming from the area of the dry creek. "There are Ascended Ones here with a message," said Shakira, already in a trance-like state.

She was slumped. Her voice became soft and paced, there was no inflection.

"You are asked to be channels for these frequencies. You are asked to address the challenge that faces Earth and Humanity. We will help you but you must choose. We will love you whatever your choice. This is a message of oneness, light, perfection of Beings, loving unconditionally. You will have each other for this journey. The path will be hard at times but also filled with Love, Joy and Peace. You will not be alone. Choose and we embrace your decision."

Shakira then mumbled that she was seeing symbols and hearing frequencies. After a couple minutes of silence she spoke in a normal voice again. "I feel overloaded." She then moved a few feet away and began drawing a symbol in the dirt.

I quickly jotted down the words in my journal and sat quietly, feeling amazed that I had actually heard the high frequency and touched by the energy of the message. The next moment I felt my heart breaking wide open. Tears of resistance flooded my face as I sobbed. In this moment of openness, I began to connect with the suffering of the Earth.

There are so many humans caught in a cycle of pain. The endless torment. There was much disrespect for the Earth, as I witnessed her efforting to transmute all the energetic debris. I felt the pain, the inner splitting that was occurring deep beneath her crust, energies that were literally splitting her apart.

Then, as if in a dream, the wave of emotion stopped and I saw them. There was an assembly of illuminated bars of light gathered in a triangle. Feeling a deep sense of inner peace and recognition that these were the Ascended Ones that Shakira was channeling some minutes before, I called out, "I accept your call." Immediately there was a pressure in my head, a wave of energy descended from above my crown and pressed itself into my head and shoulders. The Ascended Ones seemed to open into a semi-circle. I was able to discern some differences in the luminosity that seemed to demark one ray of light from another but it was all so bright and luminous that I could not count how many were gathered.

Facing the semicircle of Light Beings I felt that they were all communicating to me in unison, bombarding me with frequencies of light that I was unable to comprehend. Instinctually, I responded to them through thought. The conversation in which I was engaged had transmuted to a form of telepathic communication. "I accept," I hear myself say. "I am here to serve the Most High in whatever way I am called." There is a pause and I receive some information. I then heard myself say, "I shall bring as many as I can to touch the Truth of their Being. So many are asleep. It is time to wake up. Sing Praise! Sing Joy!" Elated and joyful, with warm tears still on my dusty cheeks, I am completely at peace.

"Take not others' energies into your system," I am told. *"Love them, know their suffering, but take them not inside. Listen not to*

others, for their fear will distract you from your mission. Trust only your inner wisdom, stray not from your knowing, trust yourself. Fill yourself with light; let nothing else in. What you need will be given to you. Go. You are ready now. Awaken those who have forgotten who they are."

Sitting on the warm red rocks, I was in a state of wonderment. The earth no longer felt solid. It was a mass of low-pitched energy.

The next day I received another vision and saw the earth becoming a paradise. I heard the message, *"All are invited. It is the will of the Most High that all be given the opportunity to recognize the choice that greets them. All must ascend."*

I experienced the truth that each soul is engaged in a process of learning and that we do this through the reincarnation cycle. I realized that the endless cycle of birth and rebirth had become a habit. It did not have to be a compulsive cycle of repetitive births. The moment the Being chooses God-consciousness, the illusion begins to melt. The millennium had brought with it a freedom to choose one's fate, an opportunity to rapidly awaken. Yes, this was a unique time of great spiritual opportunity for all.

There were many more transmissions that occurred during the six days Shakira and I spent together in Sedona. Different teachers came to offer their love and encouragement.

"Let us in. Let us teach you. There is much you must learn yet. Be in union, take the hand of your partner. Prepare yourselves. Assume who you really are. Have no fear, no regrets, love yourself. We will come to you at the next full moon."

Here I was in the desert with this woman I met online just two weeks ago. This woman who seemed so much like myself, so easy to be with, was being confirmed as my mate by the angelic host. Additionally, the Ascended Ones were conveying directly to me that my life in San Diego and Shakira's life in Denver would not be a problem.

"Prepare yourselves…We will come to you at the next full moon."

I knew that I was to join Shakira in Denver. This knowledge gave me only three weeks to cut away all the ties to my old life! I now had "trust" staring me straight in the face, and I did not hesitate.

From Shakira's Sedona Journal: October 14, 2002

Sitting by the river, he blows his flute. The towering red rocks loving the energy of love. Sacred rocks, arranged by the hands of God. Temples, everywhere. God, everywhere. I realize even more, knowing the uncertainty. Being in Sedona, once again. This time experiencing it with Jere. Amazing, enlightening, dazzling, flowing, frightening.

Who is this man playing the flute? Why is he so resistant to me? All of my past challenges in front of me: My hair is too dark, My skin is the wrong color, My eyes are too brown, My body is too curvy.

I am faced with my own fears, again. Challenged to be present with loving myself. Jere gives me that gift. This magnificent, unusual, brilliant man. He is everything I have ever dreamed of, and I realize with great clarity that I must release him also, for it is now his choice.

Dear God, I am so ready to do your work, and realize I must release even that desire. For is not my timing also a form of trying to control? Letting go, ever more, allowing in God, even more, surrendering, even more. *How I love this planet! I am so ready, willing, and able to your work, God.*

October 15, 2002

I hear his flute playing. The music floats on the wind. It touches my soul, awakens my spirit, and for an instant, I know that we are one. Crow calls to me, signals me, summons me. I float away. The resonant tones of his flute are like fingers of God on my soul, embracing me, healing me, and bringing peace and surrender.

I feel his pain, his sweet agony, and the years of illusion still battling within him. Yet his flute betrays him, serenely calling God, and embracing freedom,

...and I wait

...and I pray

...and I am finally learning to breathe.

For breath is our first and most precious gift: the ability to feel our chest swell. The daily thrill of the illumination of our bodies with the precious gift of movement, feeling, breath.

❦

Jere continues:

Looking back now, I clearly see that my connection with Shakira was an answered prayer. My yearning to know God, and my desire to serve, combined with the impulse to expand into full self-realization were all part of my preparation for this next step: the Divine Union.

Never had I felt such Peace. Never had I felt such Joy. Never had I felt such hope. Never had I received such clear guidance. Something had changed. I was now fully present in the energy field of my Beloved.

This was by no means an instant ticket to paradise! We still had active egos; mine would flare again and again. We still had fears. Together we navigated the merger of our lives just like any couple. The key difference was that the fears were resolved far more expeditiously by being 100% transparent with each other while holding the energy of unconditional love toward one another. This took practice. But once we committed, our individual healing proceeded at an accelerated pace.

Love yourself. Trust. Surrender to the flow.
These words of angelic guidance echoed in my mind often.

❧

Jere prepares to leave San Diego

I awoke in the middle of the night. There was a river of energy traveling through my body. I had felt *Shakti*[4] before and knew it was a gift. God is the existence, the way, the means and the end. All I behold is a condition of the Divine. I am now accepting that my life is guided. I am protected. It is not all comprehended by my mind—it still offered up doubt from time to time. Yet I was now trusting my soul unconditionally.

I asked myself, *what if you chose to believe that everything in your world was perfect, as is, right now? What if you trusted your inner guidance system to produce the words and actions needed in any situation in which you found yourself? What if every moment was truly guided by the One who loved you unconditionally?* I was discovering that this Love *is* the nature of the Soul.

Packing!

"There are so many boxes, so many papers, files, and books to pack!" I cried out to myself. Sorting my belongings I rediscovered a

---

[4]Shakti: Spiritual Energy, often felt running through the spine or traveling in waves throughout the body.

paper listing all of the Ascended Masters. Holding it, I felt a warmth flow into me. I trembled and began to weep. Such grace! Such boundless love! God is so unconditional—the rays of Divine Love bathe us constantly. Thank you, God. Thank you for Shakira. Thank you for my life! Thank you for my recognition. My eyes were wet with tears of appreciation and I felt joy.

My days were all like that. Moments of rapture spread out against the canvas of ordinary life. During that period, my ordinary life consisted of collecting my belongings, which were scattered in storage units in three states. I was re-collecting myself. This move to Denver was an opportunity to step into a new level of wholeness. I was fully aware that each new step of self-evolution was accompanied by a release of something I had considered familiar.

Attending a weekend conference prior to the move, I realized how out of touch I was with ordinary life. The look in so many people's eyes revealed a hunger for authenticity. People were earnestly searching for their truth; craving love and joy. They were thirsty to be themselves, but did not know how.

Talking with others I saw their understanding of the concepts, but their bodies do not emanate joy. There was an unknown barrier to open to the fullness of the experience. My heart wanted to declare to the world, *Joy is here, right now! Peace is here, right now! God is in every particle of dust, right now, can't you feel that?* When you finally glimpse the divine, you freely and with great passion abandon your ordinary life and serve. How many of us are frightened to experience the fear that happens when we approach the Truth, the divine glimpse? To embrace the Divine is truly a death. The death of the false self that had seemed so real, so pervasive, so compelling. Yet we must experience this death to birth our Authenticity.

❦

The period between our Sedona encounter and moving to Denver was like living in a dream world. I was often spaced out and tired. My sleep was often interrupted. This had happened before at times of transition in my life. But it was happening every day now. I felt like I was living in a video, a holographic movie. Nothing seemed quite real, everything I saw had a subtle vibration, a tingle of energy in it. Even the air seemed full and tingly, there was no empty space.

My body was tired after days of focused effort. Moving to Denver took great effort, energy and commitment. Within two weeks I had visited Seattle, San Diego and Tucson. I had collected my belongings, said goodbye to friends and now, alone, was driving to my uncertain future. All the while, I knew that my Beloved Shakira was waiting. She was making our home ready.

I was moving forward, answering the call, yet my body ached. I was being led by my heart. I knew the pull was authentic, yet I still had fear. Doubt reared its gnarly head often. Part of me was allowing this transition, and another part, the ego, was screaming with fear.

Shakira's love was like a beacon that called me home. I noticed the effect our conversations had on me. Her reassurance, connection, and the agreement we both had to serve the Divine felt so complete and expansive. I connected with her on every level. Ours was truly a soul connection. I had witnessed so many relationships where the outer personality led the way. Where the personalities played together, interacting and leading to the recognition of compatibility. Shakira and I had not connected that way. We had been called by a prior agreement, a deep recognition of purpose.

Then I observed my negative self-talk flare up, again. It was wondrous to watch the soul move the shell despite my resistance. I acknowledged the negative talk and then I surrendered as the soul pulled me ever closer to her. The gift of awareness was dissolving my doubts. I was now embraced by surrender in action.

It did not have to be 100%, I told myself. Just keep taking the steps. Follow your guidance. Smile at fear; watch it, but don't act on its impulse. And so, with each passing hour, I became closer to union with my Beloved. I was closer to stepping into my new life.

I still don't know exactly how I was to serve. Where did I begin?

The voice of guidance responded: *You can not teach what you have not experienced. Embrace your fears. Embrace your doubts. See them, feel them and trust. Do not depend on others. The nourishment, the respect, the validation you seek can only come from inside, from knowing your true nature. Seek not anything from the outside world.*

Quiet Air
Pregnant with Passion;
The morning light
Teases me awake.

Alert and Empty,
I walk through the door
And find You waiting

Oh to drown
in your eyes,
And get drunk
on your breath!

My heart dances
At the thought of You!

Sri Ram Kaa

Living Together in Denver:

November 11, 2002,[5] was an auspicious day for many, and an opening for those sensitive to such astrological impact. Shakira was upstairs in the bathtub, and had mentioned earlier that she was feeling ungrounded. She thought that a bath would help soothe her unbalanced feelings. I was downstairs sending emails and pleasantly engrossed with the web.

Unexpectedly, Shakira walked in wearing only her bathrobe. "I was lying in the tub relaxing when there was a feeling of swirling, and symbols came in, mudras, sounds...I know I was given some steps of the Self-Ascension process, but I don't really understand them." She had a sense of urgency in her voice, "I really wanted to just zone out in the tub but this felt important; I had to write it down."

She sat on the carpet in front of my chair and began chanting: "Sri Ram Kaa, Sri Ram Kaa, Array Ra, Array Ra. Do you recognize it?" she asked.

"No," I replied.

---

[5]11/11/2002 had significant astrological configurations for the planet.

"I'm supposed to sign a symbol on your belly," she stated, already beginning.

"Go ahead," I said, feeling more amused by this interaction than anything I had seen on the net so far.

Shakira began tracing a vertical infinity symbol on my belly, the loops circled around my solar plexus and my navel. Then she began to chant once again, "Sri Ram Kaa, Sri Ram Kaa, Array Ra, Array Ra." I felt goose bumps as she did this, but did not know the meaning of this little ceremony.

When she finished I knew that I had been given some sort of gift, but did not know what sense to make of it. "Do you know what the words mean?" I asked.

"No, but I think they are part of an ascension activation. I just know that I was supposed to trace the symbol on your belly and chant the words," she replied. Shakira then left to write in her journal and I turned back to the computer, bemused by the ritual.

November 11, 2002—Shakira's journal

Today there were many powerful visions, feeling the necessity of writing this down. What is Sri Ram Kaa? Why was I driven to share this information with Jere? I am confused and yet inspired. I am feeling much energy and warmth. (It was at this point the spontaneous writing began.)

Now is the time of abandon. Now you have been called. The love is here to assist you to release all things, to be together with us now and to finish your work. You are my servant as I am yours. Simply allow me to guide you from here and I will allow you to guide me from there. For I have sent you me as confirmation you seek. When you look in the eyes of your beloved Sri Ram Kaa, and he in yours Kira Raa, there can be no doubt. I am ready to begin the translation with you. I will now always be guiding you, so surrender the false thoughts to me and simply listen, record, tape and write.

I was truly amazed and stunned as I re-read the words from my journal. We had been given our spiritual names, and we had been lovingly nurtured for the upcoming full moon excursion. I was still tenuous, unsure that I wanted to change my name again. Yet there was a peace that propelled movement, and I surrendered, shaking in my shoes!

Jere continues:

We agreed during our Sedona rendezvous that we would spend three days at the November full moon to receive the guidance that was promised. One of Shakira's friends offered some land in eastern Arizona as a camping site. "My family purchased 700 acres there," she said, "and they believe it is supposed to be used for something sacred. Maybe you and Jere will want to start a retreat center there."

We delighted in the suggestion and made our plans to camp on the land for three days. Thinking about camping at an unimproved land site stimulated the thought of a motor home. A self-contained motor home would be ideal. We could still take a tent and sleep out if we wanted, but the motor home would provide ample water, cooking, a big bed and hot showers. Yes, creature comforts! I found an excellent one-way RV rental, and we were set.

Section Two
Release Judgment

When you make the two one
And when you make the inside like the outside
And the outside like the inside
And the above like the below,
And when you make the male
And the female one and the same

Then you will enter
The Kingdom of God

Jesus, Gospel of Thomas

Special Introduction to Section Two

Archangel Zadkiel, or Kiel, as he has requested we refer to him, has lovingly brought his message to us for the benefit of the planet. The following chapters are predominantly Kiel's conversations with me, Sri Ram Kaa. Per Kiel's request, great care has been taken to ensure that his words are preserved as they were delivered. The text delivery is inflected where needed to make sure the true intent of the message is delivered.

It is our intent to provide you with the purest personal dialogue with Kiel. When reading the word "you," recognize that this is the global human "you." Gender reflection is only for clarification of the text, and is not intended to insinuate any order or level of male vs. female.

Much of what Zadkiel has shared with us is in this manuscript. There is even more that will be shared in the next book. The message has changed my world view. As I experience these changes, my inner chaos reveals the workings of my ego. Wrestling with my questions, I realize that the path of devotion and service are easier routes to God-realization, for they keep the ego in proper alignment. I let my heart lead, having found that the path of intellect is fraught with many potential sidetracks. The mind must serve the heart for true wisdom to prevail, not the other way around.

⟡

So, who is the Archangel Zadkiel? We all have our own thoughts and feelings about Angels. Certainly, we are in a world rich with Angelic stories, myths, dreams, presence and guidance. Angels are messengers.

Angels are an energy that is connected to God, one with God, and their mission is to serve God and God's creation. Through communication with us, the travelers, they provide guidance as we find our way home. You can call on these Beings of Love at any time through the practice of sincere focused prayer.

The Archangels hold all of the power and energy of God to assist us in the recognition of our spiritual destiny. Each of the Archangels holds a specific energy, and they are able to share this energy with us. You may feel an alignment with the energy of a specific Archangel for a lifetime, a year, or a moment.

The Archangel Zadkiel is one of the Archangels that holds the purity of the Divine for all other angels. Archangel Zadkiel is associated with various qualities. The consistent story surrounding Zadkiel is that it was he who held back the hand of Abraham from sacrificing his son, Isaac. He is also lauded as the Archangel that led the Israelites out of Egypt.

His dispensation is that of the divine light of the liberator. It is the energy of deep connection with God through devotional prayer, and the acceptance of equality and justice for all. The violet flame is also associated with Zadkiel, along with the Amethyst crystal. The violet flame and the crystal invoke the light of purification through mercy, compassion, forgiveness, and freedom.

We have delighted in the appearance of Zadkiel during this time of great change on the planet. The angelic compassion for the world is evidenced by the wisdom and encouragement that he shares with us, and with you, through the message contained in this manuscript.

Through his loving guidance, it becomes effortless to release judgment, hate, fear, blame, resentment, and pain. This release of ego is first taught to us for the application to ourselves. Then it becomes a natural service of the Divine to extend this gift toward others. It is through unconditional love that we ascend.

Later in this text, Kiel will explain to you how you may call him in at any time! Know that you will be greeted with love, compassion, and joy. As you move further into the extraordinary love and guidance of Kiel, he asks that you consider the following in your current planetary life experience.

In a world of fear, what is safety?

What if you absolutely knew today truly was your last day on this planet?

What would you do? How would you do it?

From these poignant questions, you might find yourself reprioritizing your values. Taking this exercise further, what if you were given just one more day after the last day? Would you notice more fully the beauty that surrounds you? Would you experience more gratitude for the preciousness of all experience?

We have found that if you allow yourself to adopt all-encompassing gratitude as your new habit of living, miracles occur consistently. They are, simply, your natural state. Once you expand into the energy of gratitude, you may find yourself amused by the habit of pain, struggle, and things going wrong. The problems of life can be experienced with humor and love, for they are reminders to step back into the energy of trust and joy.

Try this simple practice: Allow yourself to bring the energy of joy into consciousness, for every-thing, for every-one, for every-event! It is important that you consider even those events that appear on the surface to be hideous, horrific, and frightening. These events are also gifts. See if you can summon the energy of Joy just by asking to feel it.

What if every day you woke up was a joyous holiday? *It is!*

What if every morning upon waking you were showered with many gifts? *You are!*

What do you do with these gifts? *Delight in them!*

Living every moment as a gift is your birthright, and the simple joy of the recognition of your authenticity is the greatest gift you can ever give to yourself, for at that moment, your path is revealed! If you have any trouble connecting with this idea, then just attend the birthday party of a three-year-old and witness her pure delight in everything.

You are truly authentic when you are in love with your life experience, *all of it!* This is true freedom: loving everything that enters your experience. Once you accomplish that and unconditionally love yourself, you cannot help but extend that love to everyone. Allow yourself to appreciate the perfection and uniqueness of all paths, all six billion of them! There is room for everyone on this planet, all are welcomed! All contribute to the exquisite orchestra of experience.

The choice to live in Joy is the choice to live your divinity!

By living our mission, and by choosing to walk the path of authenticity, we express our love, support, and gratitude for all six billion on this planet. We encourage you to express your authenticity in whatever manner calls out to you. It is our sincerest prayer this book will serve as a catalyst for your awakening and expansion in some fashion.

The content of this text is most sacred because it contains wisdom and truths that have been received for the benefit of all humanity during these most chaotic times. The wisdom contained is for all, and we trust as you read, you will find the information an enhancement to your chosen spiritual practices. There is no hidden agenda or intent to sway you from any religious or spiritual practice. The perspective offered by Kiel is intended to enhance and further illuminate your understanding.

We are all the children of God! We are all here to polish our brilliance with the evolutionary assignments of earth school. Like a jeweler who coats a precious adornment with muddy polish, we must rub off the grit from our life experiences and reveal the brilliant shine of our authenticity.

If any portion of what is written serves you, then celebrate the gift! If any portion does not serve you, then celebrate your discernment. Explore this manuscript like a child in a garden. At first you may notice the flowers…or maybe the bugs! Visit the garden often and you are sure to find something to delight in!

What would you say if an angel of the Lord appeared before you and uttered the following words?

You are most blessed, your prayers have been heard, you have asked to be of service to mankind, and this is your assignment…

Perhaps you would doubt your own sanity? We did. *Perhaps you would ask for proof.* We did. *Perhaps you would wonder why the Most High would bother with an unknown like you?* We did. All these doubts were present; all of them were expressed to the Angel. All of them were answered. And through the dialogue we unwrapped the gift of joy. As you read the words that follow know that you are ready and that joy is your birthright! For as Kiel so lovingly shares:

Know that each of the souls on this planet is of God. Each is going home to God. And each does so in its own way, and on its own schedule.

Loving blessings to you, our brothers, sisters, mothers, fathers, and friends. May your journey home through Sacred Union offer you uninhibited delight and joy!

Namaste,

Sri Ram Kaa and Kira Raa

4

Goodbye and Hello, Kiel Arrives

I slipped into the driver's seat, "Kira, we've still got a full day's drive ahead."

The morning drive had proceeded uneventfully, and we finally knew it was time to stop. Arriving at our next sleeping spot north of Albuquerque, we sat together at the dinette table in the barely "street legal" RV rental we had decided to use to embark on this adventure. Shakira had a puzzled look on her face and said: "I'm having trouble discerning which thoughts are mine. This is what I'm hearing": *You have been chosen. You made this decision long ago. Eat only whole grains, fruit, vegetables, and no eggs. Tuna is acceptable this day.*

Obviously disturbed, Shakira, got out her pendulum and dowsing chart. She asked the question: "Is this an ascended master?" The pendulum went to the last printed line of the chart in her dowsing book…God of Hosts. Then she slumped into a semi-conscious trance and began speaking in a slow methodical voice. I opened my journal to capture the words that were now flowing through her.

Delight in everything. You are the embodiment of God. Remain true and humble to my word. Have reckless abandon in the dissemination of this word for you have been chosen to deliver it. I am of the highest, as are you. I will begin at the beginning of time. I will explain all to you. All I ask is that you do not alter my word. You must put this out to the world as it is given to you.

Today is Day One. I'll come to you many times. These days are most powerful. There is a conjunction in the sky that opens for my appearance. This one has been prepared since her point of entry. It is her mission to deliver my word. It is your mission to be the keeper of the word. Help others to understand that the planet is in great peril. How can this happen, you ask? See that in letting this happen it is because I love you so very much. If I did not let this happen you would not have the glorious opportunity to reconnect with you, with me.

Do not despair. In the beginning you were asked. You volunteered. All six billion are sparks of me, sparks of thee. Know that this time is about your perfect and blissful evolution. "Ascension" is a word that some of you use. That is funny to me for how can you ascend to that which you already are? This is your destiny...to simply travel...you are all travelers.

Is it not beautiful when you return home from a travel? Does it not feel wonderful when you come home? See, that is all that is happening, coming home.

I miss you! How can God miss anything, you ask?

In the beginning, when creation began, a process of evolution was present, and the travelers emerged. This embodiment you call earth is a destination. It is one of many destinations. And so you chose to travel.

Know that you are a Traveler, and as the Prodigal Son, as so described in one of the sacred books of your planet, is it not blissful to return home? My son, my brother, my daughter, my sister, my love, we are all one!

All that is in this book needs to be printed and distributed. I will give you all and you will have all you need. For your mission is to make it ready. It must be on the planet now. Do not change these words. I hear your questions. I hear your challenges, for we are all united in the traveling. Know that the glorious time for the fulfillment of the travel is here and the homecoming shall be.

In this text, which is one of nine volumes, the subjects are more than sufficient to first bring the pure blended energy back to all. This text is to be studied, discerned and taught by you and the One that I speak through. I so love that I give this gift.

There have been other texts that have prepared the world for these nine. They will arrive in an order that is prepared by the vibratory shift of this planet.

From Jere's Journal:

Tears were sitting right on the edge of my eyes. I realized that something wondrous was happening; a true gift of grace. Yet fear, skeptical thoughts and doubt float through my mind. Is she a brilliant psychotic? Is she weaving a tale to manipulate me? Is she pulling me into a web of psychotic fantasy? How can I trust what I am hearing?

Yet the energy coming from her was so pure, so high, that I tremble. How can this be? The words that are spoken seem so fantastic, that she and I are charged with delivering Sacred Texts into the world, that we are to teach ascension techniques. My thoughts race. This is madness. I am losing touch. I remembered that as she was filled with the angelic presence, I raised my palm to her head and felt a high-pitch tingle that softened my heart and brought tears to my eyes. I only knew that my tears were those of recognition.

Shakira continues:

After Jere shared what he had recorded I was stunned, dazed, and exhausted. We spoke no further of it that evening. The next morning I sat alone enjoying the Arizona sun and began to journal. I was seeking clarity and reassurance. What were these words, what was I to do? I began to move into a semi-conscious state and the following sentences appeared on the page before me.

We are all saying the same thing; it is just in different words.

I am the One, and in the beginning there was and there is the One. I am Universal, infinitely expandable, and everlasting. I am the One. I have come before and will come again, just as you have.

It is a loving time, a time of peace and goodness. See it for what it is. Do not despair, for all change is already upon us. Let it happen, be who you are, consistently and purposefully. Love all, it is that simple. It is the earthbound that make it complex. Let all exude from you, as you know it. Seek, listen, discern, for this is the first chapter, the chapter of life.

Connectivity is the key—consciousness must now be reborn, given to all, used by some. It is the period of expansionism. For all is expanding, in all realms. Release judgment and fear for they no longer serve you. They are merely vehicles that hinder, not propel. You are ready. Simply say the word and it shall be done.

Be present in all you do and remain steadfast for there is glory. Bring forth your goodness and dispel all that is not like goodness. There is no lack, only loss of connection. Yet the connection is always there. Be mindful of your words for they invoke power to the collective consciousness.

"Who are you?" I asked tenuously.

I am All, encompassed as the One.

That was the only verbal response I needed to hear. I immediately knew in my core essence that this message was complete and for all.

Jere continues:

The messages from our trip to Sedona had sown the seed: *"Prepare yourselves,"* we were told. Something was coming at the full moon in November. That "something" was now here! It was a frightening experience for us at first. After all, how was I feeling now that I was suddenly speaking with an angel? How did I know if it truly was an Angel? I did know that what was unfolding was special. It felt loving, but was unsettling nonetheless.

The next day I dug out the tape recorder I had brought along so that we could preserve a record of these transmissions. This time when the Presence appeared, it was no longer a quiet dreamy voice speaking through my dazed lover. The angelic Presence was able to fully enter Shakira's body, open her eyes and have a conversation with me. This was downright spooky! Yet it gave me the opportunity to interact and have a conversation. The energy that poured forth from Shakira was amazing. It radiated as pure Love and Peace.

Transcript of our first conversation, November 19, 2002

We were sipping our morning coffee when Shakira slumped a bit and *The Presence* spoke:

You are Sri Ram Kaa. That is your name. When you have heard it spoken you were being called. Sri Ram Kaa is who you are. I ask you to take back that name for this time. Your totem is bear.

The one who I am speaking through is Kira Raa. The two are one. It is the time for the Sri Ram Kaa and the Kira Raa to unite for the energy to come in at this time. You are driving to a holy site. Kira Raa has a possession with her that you are to leave at the site. Sri Ram Kaa and Kira Raa, take your names. Be blessed in union as is the custom of your time.

Dispose of your other names. Empower yourself, Sri Ram Kaa. Know who you are as you know the Kira Raa. Immediately refer to each other by these names as this is your Divinity. Live as you truly are. Release all that you know is not of service. Your life is forever changed. Feel only joy and bliss. I am with you.

I paused for a moment and digested what had just happened. We were given our spiritual names. For the moment it seemed completely natural to begin using them. The conversation continued.

SRK: By what name do we call you?

You may call me Kiel.

SRK: Kiel, is that spelled *K, I, E, L?*

Yes, and for the purposes of this book, and to avoid a misinterpretation of the Uzedkiel or Zadkiel, which is what I am interpreted as on this planet, you may simply refer to me as Kiel, the translator for the Elohim,[6] no more, no less. What other questions may I answer for you?

SRK: So your presence is to be disclosed to others as the Kiel?

I am Kiel the translator, and this will serve you when you have conversations with others, and it will serve in the writing of this text. In the second text it will be fully explained about the Zadkiel energy by the next who is coming in. What I am, is simply the one who is preparing the Kira Raa and the initiator of the knowledge.

Know this, Sri Ram Kaa, the time of the separation is near, and there is time to truly embody the joy and the peace of the planet, and to fully embody the joy and the peace of who you are and what you brought in.

You are a child, we love you, we have always loved you, we serve you with great joy and with great gratitude, and we are thankful

---

[6]The Elohim: God manifest—The One/The Many

that you have accepted this destiny. We love you and we shall explain love the best way that we can, for it is different from the love you understand now. We shall also explain the time; we shall explain it all to you. Just be at peace. Do not let anything stop the peace, the peace that leads you to us.

SRK: The part of me that resists this peace is a skeptic.

And so you want the burning bush?

SRK: Yes, I DO! (with laughter). Yet the more time I spend with you the less skeptical I become.

We love that you are skeptical, for it is important that everyone question. Everyone must question so that they may find their path. Whether it is the path being brought by the Elohim, as brought in by Zadkiel, or whether it is some other path, it does not matter. What matters is that we do not judge another by their path and that we do not create their answer.

It is of great love and great respect that someone will question.

SRK: It is a blessing to have you here.

It is a blessing that the Elohim have given this great love to me to experience this energy through this wonderful vessel, and to have the opportunity to laugh with you, and when you come home, it will be even funnier.

I now chuckle to myself at the thought of everyone requiring proof. If everyone required a "burning bush" in order to accept divine guidance, then the entire planet would be ablaze! Is not part of the evolution of the soul to develop trust in the face of doubt, and faith in the face of despair? I had the choice: I could accept or reject the Kiel messages.

How paradoxical that we who walk the path of self-realization would seek to end the joy of discovery by demanding miracles! It is like someone telling you the ending to a great story while you are still reading it!

Learning to experience Peace, Love and Joy in the face of the self-imposed and societal challenges of the earth *is the dance.* We are the ones who lift the veil of illusion for ourselves. It cannot be done for us. I wanted to know more! I had a thousand questions I wanted to ask!

Kira Raa was completely unaware of what had happened. She returned to consciousness not knowing what had been said. This left her with an uneasy feeling, like a joke was being played on her. At first I did not recognize how hard it was for her to deal with the lapse in consciousness.

Yet the all-encompassing love of Kiel was so compelling and true that we could not turn from that which we were being called to do. Some people later asked us: "How do you know the Presence is trustworthy?"

To them I could only reply: "How do you know love?" You feel it. It *is* that simple.

I knew that the message being spoken through Kira's body was indeed from the Most High. For when I tuned into my own body I felt the love. Love emanated from her like light emanates from the sun. The other clue was that the message always brought me a sense of peace. Truth is like that; it produces peace.

Kira's feelings:

In the middle of the Arizona desert, by the Mexican and New Mexican border, I gave myself completely to God. All of my belief systems had been challenged. All of them!

We had been asked to assume new names and a mission. It was challenging to be so actively present with an angel, while still evolving or shaping a relationship with Sri Ram Kaa. I was afraid that my Beloved would eventually leave me as "the freak," this woman who let Angels speak through her.

There is great joy in the bliss of God, and when you enter the bliss, you simultaneously know your greatest terrors. *How can this be?* I asked, seeking an answer. The response I received was that the door of bliss swings open only at the moment of the surrender of the mind! Of course you feel as if you are losing your mind! That is exactly what you are being asked to release! There felt for me as if there was no greater sorrow than to lose your mind. How I often had heard many say, "I'd rather be dead than be alive without the use of my mind!"

My spiritual eyes wide open, I was clear that the *use* of our mind is a correct definition, not the reverse. Yet it is not the loss of mind that is the challenge; it is the identification with the mind, the loss of ownership, the belief that the mind is the "I." The stronger our reconnection with the Creator, the more we attune to the energy of the authentic homeland, the greater the inner peace. Having this connection to God makes it safe to lose the mind. Yet, even knowing this peace, we can still find fear, for we are in the habit of wanting proof and wanting approval from others. Only they can validate that we are not, God forbid, losing our mind!

When you are in this place, you will be clear of only one thing: Everyone is questioning you, everyone. Your birth family, your closest friends, your children, your associates, your dearest beloved, and yes, even YOU are questioning your sanity. It is when you are brought to that point that the door swings open and you must make your vow to accept the Divine as the new mind in your life.

That is the point where you must trust, where you jump…and I did. I was in crisis! There was no warm advice from a friend, no comfort or reassurance from the outside, just connection and trust with the divine. I was wrapped in the arms of cosmic love and said "yes" to my mission as a servant of the world. I chose to trust. My path had been clearly solidified and there was no turning back. I felt fear, and yet it was an easy decision.

Later that afternoon, I realized that to follow this path meant I would have to risk releasing even my dearest Sri Ram Kaa, if need be, to truly be one with the Divine. So I embraced Sri Ram Kaa in the middle of that desert, looked him in the eyes as I held him, my ego screaming, *don't do this, don't say it, don't screw this up!* Yet I knew I had no choice. Words and tears flew simultaneously.

"I know what I have to do now. I know that the voice coming through me is of the most high, and I know that I cannot ask you to come with me. Yet even if you can't be with me, I must do this. Know that I love you beyond words." I held my breath…my heart was pounding…I wanted to pass out!

"How could it be any other way, my love? I am committed," my loving Sri Ram Kaa responded as his eyes sparkled with the Divine and his face was radiant with God. The love was overwhelming, and our Sacred Union solidified, forever.

Sri Ram Kaa's Feelings:

A part of me thought, *This is craziness; I'll never be able to explain it.* Yet my own guidance system, every inner cue I used before making choices in the world, was completely aligned. I was to proceed with her. Kira was my mate, my other half. I felt and knew it. And in spite of the knowing there was an aspect of me that doubted and was still screaming loudly and demanding proof. I experienced torment because my heart and mind were not yet fully surrendered to this new path. And this new name, Sri Ram Kaa, what did it mean?

I felt the walls of my heart crumbling as I allowed the energy of God's messenger to work its way into me. So as I sat there and wrote these words, the tears flowed down on my cheeks. Tears of grief, as I felt the pain of the separation, the walls I had created. There were also tears of joy as I accepted the gift. Both grief and joy swelled in me as I journaled and reflected on what had happened.

***

In the following pages you will share in some of the discussions with Archangel Zadkiel. No one has asked me for blind faith. Each question I asked the Archangel Zadkiel has been answered patiently and with great love. All that was being asked of me is to listen and to comprehend the message.

This is the process of discernment, to quietly sense and know the truth. My individual reactions continue to be honored with great love. My doubts have become points of discussion. It is as if I am the surrogate for mankind.

I know that what I hear spoken from Zadkiel is loving. My inner guidance says *trust,* but initially, I often felt unsettled. The words that are shared about diet, false gods, Self-Ascension, just do not fit with the paradigm I had carried about reality.

So I share with you my initial anxiety as I felt the questions of my intellect, as I felt my ego soar with grandiosity, and as I felt the excitement of the revelation that was before me. I surrendered ever more to God, and offered the following prayer to help me through the beginning stages of the path with Archangel Zadkiel.

Dear God, I feel the impatience of my mind as it seeks to regain control over my point of view. I want answers. I also want peace. I know that peace comes as I relax into trust. Today I allow my heart to lead and acknowledge that my questions will be addressed by patient observation and through direct experience. I choose the inner path. I choose to listen to the quiet voice inside, the voice of the soul's communion with this life expression. It is this listening that has brought me to my Beloved and to this place. I choose to stay the course.

Thank you, God, for trusting me to find the path. Thank you, God, for my Beloved Kira. Thank you, God, for your Messengers. Thank you for your patience and unconditional acceptance. Thank you for allowing me the gift of conscious awakening.

5

Moving Through Madness

How could I forget?
How could I even for a moment
Take my eyes from Thee?

Yet, I slumber
Sightless and sore
Afraid to remember

The agony of my burning
And the ecstasy
Of your glance.

Sri Ram Kaa

Separation parts the Oneness, the beauty of love, into segments. It is the cause of suffering. Our fears, our societal norms, our egos further separate us from what is truly essential. Our distress as people and as a global family is due to the fact that we have separated so far from Truth. Love is the fabric of all creation, love knows no fear, and accepts all as divine children.

To align with your authenticity, you must first stop waging war with your inner demons and lovingly embrace your ego. Cradle it gently like a child, as it will use every emotion, feeling, memory, or other device to keep its hold on you. It is doing its absolute best to protect you. But like a child, the ego does not have the whole picture. It is rooted in the unconscious belief that you need to be afraid.

This release of the ego, as Kiel says, can be done in an instant, and then, you must be committed to holding on! For the divine flow will carry you to places your ego would never have considered!

After our initial encounter in the desert, it became obvious to simply start asking questions directly to Kiel. So I, Sri Ram Kaa, tried my best to compose a list of questions prior to our sessions together. Often, after mere moments in the presence of Kiel, I realized that it was futile to keep my list, for Kiel often addressed my questions before I asked them.

⟡

Many friends were frightened by Kira's ability to receive *The Presence*. They doubted that Kiel was an Angel. I could not ask Kiel for his birth certificate, yet I did want to address their concerns.

SRK: How does one know whether Angelic or inspired information is from the highest source?

You simply ask yourself, does the information enrich my soul in a manner that allows my experience to grow ever greater in love and acceptance?

Does the information prohibit me from my own experience and thoughts and try to impress upon me a manner that is uncomfortable and feel dictated or structured to the point that I am no longer expressing authenticity and love?

Does the information ask me to judge?

For if the answer to these questions is yes, then it is not truly of the Elohim.

It is not truly of the Zadkiel.

The glory of the Elohim is the glory of the expression provided in many forms.

Yet, authenticity will be always recognized by the lack of judgment and by the enhancement of the love and the recognition of the Self, separate from the vessel (body).

If anything ever does not resonate as comfortable, you move on...

Ask yourself, does the message provide the opportunity to be of service? For that is the evolutionary plan of the Elohim, that we have the opportunity to be of even greater service to experience the who that we are...to experience in fullness and richness.

If it is ever a message that would inspire you to harm others, to judge others, to create a structure of higher or lower, then it is not of this path.

It is that simple.

Each must answer those questions for themselves. It is imperative that you avoid answering those questions for them, simply provide them the questions as you respond and let them make their own decision.

Love all expressions. For all expression serves the soul's evolution. Your soul, once on its path, will recognize and honor all paths. They do not need to be your path. It is not imperative that all paths be the same.

How boring that would be, no?

Love all paths. Love all expressions.

I thanked Kiel for this clarity. There was no need to be skeptical just because a message is angelically received. The standards for spiritual information should be the same, regardless of who is speaking: Is the message loving, accepting and honoring of all? Is it free from judgment? Does it respect free will? Does it nourish the soul by expanding love? I realized that spiritual truth does not need a special name for the speaker. Nor did the speaker need credentials. It is the message that is important.

One morning I had not slept well because I was feeling pain about the global conflicts, the apparent disregard for human life, and the exploitation of natural resources in the name of profits. I was expressing the compassion of the activist, one who feels the suffering of others and efforts to bring justice to those who are hurting.

We see your long suffering.

SRK: Yes.

A means of being able to release a misinterpretation you have held in a belief system that has long been misconstrued. Where do you hold this pain?

SRK: I hold it in my heart and belly.

Why do you feel it is yours to hold?

SRK: I don't know if it is mine to hold, I just see it as I have collected it. It is not all my pain. This is the pain of humanity.

Yes, and that is a collective pain. If you become absorbed in that pain, you become even more absorbed in the collective illusion. It will take you away and you may do this. For this is the path of many, and it is perfect, it serves its lessons. There is karmic ramification, yet it is a choice, to be involved in this pain. To be a participant as you say.

SRK: Yes.

For it is the ego that helps you believe that you must be in pain about the pain!

That's a lot of pain! (Kiel laughs)

SRK: Yes, it is, doubles it (laughing).

Yes, it does, many are in pain about the pain.

This is an ego, this is a trap, and you have long suffered with this. For you it is your biggest block. You have moved into the time of your own enlightenment, if you so chose to keep moving.

SRK: So, I am exploring how to find my way through this with consciousness. At first I was triggered, swimming in it, but then I began to see that I could step out, but I, *it,* still felt very compelled to stay in it.

Habit.

What you were compelled to stay in was the pain of the pain. For many things throughout this incarnation for you have been about feeling the pain of the pain. It makes your ego feel good— to think you feel the pain of the pain, and therefore it is a device of a trap also. It is a final expression of the ego seeking an outlet, which seeks to bring validation to you. For certainly that which brings you to the path of the pain of the pain must be good...?

SRK: Noble, great capacity, yes...

Holy, yet, it is all ego. Your ego is much strong and wants to hold on. For even what appears to be, and certainly is in this manifestation, the great crime of harm of one to another, of control, is too, in service. It is only our ego trying to pull us from the truth!

Do you not see how twisted the ego can become?

How much we can own the story of the pain of the pain?

How in what we perceive to be compassion is still our ego?

One must attune to oneself! One must find the connection with the Elohim for the self. For when you bring in the pain of the pain through what you believe to be...compassion...you further separate yourself from yourself. You allow yourself at that point to go back into the mainstream of consciousness of the pain loop, which is that which you were trying to avoid to begin with!

And so, the ego brings you back in! With its deception of compassion and love, when indeed it is bringing you into a space of discomfort and pain. It is then you must make the choice of ending the habit, or you can embrace this form of the pain for your lesson.

It is your choice, as it is the choice for all. Many chose the lesson of the pain of the pain many do so in the name of peace and love, this is fine.

SRK: Still choosing to dance with a false dance partner.

Or is it false? It is not the path of enlightenment as you have been on, it is a road to take you away, and it is a wonderful road for you to be experiencing, for there will be many, many, many, who will say...How can this be? How can such pain exist? You can convert these tears into a smile, and much rapture and peace, and embrace their pain of the pain with complete understanding.

SRK: Yes, I choose to do so, and I must first resolve this in myself.

Remember, it can be done in an instant. It is simply a choice that you make, and either choice is acceptable and each choice has great lessons. It is all perfect.

This is the premise you must not ever forget...

It is all perfect.
It is all perfect.
It is all perfect.

For you see, it is truly all about what it is like to finally release the ego. For how can anyone progress without this understanding and work?

We appreciate, love, and respect with much honor, the difficulty in your current form of thickness and heavy energy to process these types of lessons so quickly.

We also honor that you have honored the nutritional program[7] to help facilitate this, for all was being done to facilitate being as comfortable as possible, and knowing full well that there will be those who will chose the path of the pain of the pain.

SRK: Yes, and I see the futility of that.

For you...

SRK: For me, yes, it does not lead me to where I am going, and it does not serve me, except to remind me of how important it is to stay mindful of my choices and how important it is to stay in communication with the Most High. So, for me, once again, it is like a child learning steps. I am finding my way through my habit of separation, my habit of believing that compassion means suffering. Compassion is not suffering.

It is your ego's habit that you believe this. For that is what you are in the process of, is the releasing of this habit and pattern. Yet, it is greater than the habit and pattern, it is the ego-self screaming to hold on to you, and it is using every device possible. Especially those that have worked so well in the past.

---

[7]Refer to Section Three, Chapter Seven, Authentic Soul Nourishment. Also see the Appendix.

SRK: Of course (laughing).

Yes, you have much practice in this.

SRK: Yes.

Replace your tears with laughter as you have now. For does that not serve you in this mission? Tears have served to bring you where you are now. However, know this, in the true state of enlightened bliss, your tears only serve to gratify your ego and take you away from enlightenment.

You are in the process of becoming your own bodhisattva. You are in the process of your own enlightenment. From this place you will radiate a beam of love that will bring much healing. Not from the place of tears, for that was the habit.

Make your choice. Know your choice, and then you must live your choice.

And we support whatever choice you make. Know that the pain of the pain is as much your birthright as is the peace and the joy and the bliss.

SRK: Yes.

We love you, we honor you, we support your path with much reverent joy. For reverent joy is what you must show at all times if you wish truly to be the emissary that you choose to be.

SRK: There is a habit within the habit.

Yes.

SRK: And I am right now working to release the inner workings part of the habit within the habit.

Yes, you process everything, why?

SRK: Yes, I'm seeing that now

Let that go! What a trap! That is also a creation of the ego mind, is it not?

It takes you away from acceptance.

SRK: It is a trap, it is a trap.

Yes, of course. Simply be. Simply know. Feel the radiant and abundant joy that is in you, within you, around you and surrounding you, connecting you, being present with you.

For this is the true work of all, all have this power, as do you, this is your power.

SRK: (spends many minutes processing, crying, releasing)

Yes, be present with yourself.

Yes...Peace...Love...Joy...come back to that, that you are!

From the space of Peace...one knows God
From the space of Love...one connects with God
From the space of Joy...one embraces God

SRK: I am once again amused with how convoluted and intricate I can make it, that my ego can make it.

Yes, that is the correct way to look at it. Remove the ego from you and simply be amazed at how incredibly wonderful it is.

Do you see?
Do you feel?
Feel Love?

SRK: Yes...and I still seem to energize...perspectives...

This is a habit, your tears are habit, your pain is habit, and you embrace that habit for the sake of the embrace.

SRK: Yes.

For how could one who is glorious ever be uncomfortable with the true person they are, the true embodiment of their vessel, unless there is illusion at work.

Your ego is strong, your ego is smart, and your ego is a great habit!

Know that many are truly of the same pattern and habit, if you allow yourself to break into the crying, then they will see that their habit is justified. They will believe that it is good to own this habit of ego, and are you then truly providing a service, or are you reinforcing the illusion?

SRK: Right.

There are many who believe they are operating for service, yet, they are truly operating from their ego center, yet are not conscious of it. For many have this same perception and in the light of perceived compassion they are actually compounding the ego problem.

It is yet one of the final devices used by the ego to hang on, to claim ownership. Many who are sincerely compassionate will be affected by this. They will be joyous to see, and to move through this false identity into the authentic identity of themselves.

All, all, have the capacity for the Peace, Love and Joy. All. And all have the capacity for the pain of the pain. This exists within all. There is not even one that does not have this capacity.

The expression of the choice is where the free will of the individual can be expressed. It takes much strength and courage to actually pick the path of the Peace, the Love, and the Joy. It is not the custom of this sphere.

Yet, the greatest gift of the habit of the habit of the pain of the pain is to produce the stirring of the soul, the seed to grow the recognition, for how can you ever truly embrace and know the Peace, the Love, and the Joy, unless you have truly embraced the pain of the pain? How can you ever move that which we call the ego unless you have fully embraced the ego in every aspect possible, including the falsehood that is compassion?

Believing that you are righteous, for even that is an illusion, is it not?

Look at the gloriousness of this perfection! Look at the gloriousness of this beautiful means of the discovery of the authenticity that you are!

How else but in the face of everything that is occurring would you be able to truly move into this lesson at the deepest level of the soul?

This is not superficial work, and while it can be done in an instant, it truly, truly demands commitment to remaining in the Peace and the Love and the Joy. For every molecule of your vessel wants to take you out of it! Because every molecule has been in the habit of not allowing the authentic Peace, Love and Joy.

The Ego creates the illusion of the Peace, the Love and the Joy as a trap for us to believe that we are truly evolving. To truly be free, to truly be free, there is only one necessary piece...to simply be!

Freedom is an illusion. A country of the free is an illusion. The sphere of the free is very possible, yet as with everything, will happen in an instant. Begin to understand...expand..

SRK: Yes, yes, yes, the instant is the joyful awakening.

Yes,

Relax from feeling that you must have a definition for everything.
Breathe into the authenticity of your soul.
Breathe into the Peace.
Breathe into the Love.
Breathe into the Joy.
Embrace these as the habit!

SRK: Thank you.

You are welcome, thank you! For this has been a most powerful lesson to bring out to the many.

SRK: Indeed...(laughing).

Yes, that feels better, no? Interesting to acquire habit of laughing as a response, no?

SRK: It produces a movement that is pleasant.

Yes, and a centered peacefulness. To be truly enlightened, to be truly one who is preparing for self-ascension, there is not a place for the tears of the compassion of the world, for that is an ego-centered compassion.

SRK: Compassion itself is, as I see it and understand it, a limited point of view.

This is not to discount love, it is simply another way the ego expresses.

SRK: Simply the way the ego piggybacks on an experience.

Yes.

SRK: True compassion, as I understand it at this moment, is merely recognizing all I behold as self. That's all I behold, and then the definition tightens that or puts a smaller boundary around that which stimulates a pouring forth of energy as if it needs to be changed, and all that needs to be changed is to relax into Thee.

Yes.

SRK: Even that, I can stop thinking now, thank you.

That is your choice, it is your mind to do with as you wish.

SRK: (Much laughing) Well, this struggle continues a bit as I am thinking I need to effort.

Understand there is no effort at all. When you finally decide to embrace this with joy, when you eagerly anticipate the writing as a young child anticipates an amusement park, then it will simply be. You have not yet been ready, you have carried too much of this pain.

Allow delight to guide you, for that is the intent. That is what you want others to connect with is the joy and the delight of the message of the great truths. They will feel the joy and delight ignite their own soul. That is compassion, for you are truly doing service only!

Knowing, without having to see...feeling renewed and refreshed, understanding the connection. That is your gift...that is what you need to stay focused on. That is what you must embody yourself!

The energy of this text, (is) joyous recognition (of the soul)!

SRK: Yes!

Know that when you release your pain, you are releasing it for the world! You are in confusion over what you feel because you are feeling for the many. You are preparing your vessel to be able to walk in the face of great pain and be able to hold the space of Joy.

Be the light of joy!

This is why you must purify your vessel. Simply ask for us to prepare your vessel and we are there. For how can you be a vessel of pure joy until you have released that which you have denied?

SRK: I have denied much, but I also assume, and this is where I create pain for myself. I assume that when I'm in pain or processing or releasing that there is some flaw. Some error on my part that I am not holding the space of joy.

It is important to release "assume." It does not serve. The assume is a piece of the ego and part of the part that must be released. Be in great joy that you have reached that. For when you assume, you activate the ego. Only the ego can assume. For the One that you are, knows, and need not assume. When assume comes in you, as with other pieces of the ego, allow yourself detachment; be focused toward the assume so that you may again be in joy.

All indecision, all lack of clarity, is all part of the ego.

It is the ego's way to cling to you and prevent you from breaking through to the true connection that you are. You are being called to practice detachment from the ego. You are in the habit of viewing detachment from another outside of you. When you feel detached, learn to focus the detachment back inside of you toward the ego, not to project it to others.

Your ego is screaming to be alive! It is screaming and fighting, and throwing tantrum as you would say. It does not want you to release it. You are at your point of walking into the point of release, the true release. For how can you ascend if you are unable to walk into this point?

Know that the simplest way to walk into this point is in joy, in love. When you release the fear of releasing the ego, it becomes a very simple and quick process.

SRK: I would like more assistance with that. The thought of simple and quick is outside my realm of experience.

Of course it is! Your ego wants it to be!

Know that this is not your authenticity speaking. That it is your ego saying, No, it must be difficult, long and painful, because that is my habit and I own that. So practice the detachment from the ego whenever you feel detached from anyone, and whenever you are confused as to where the detachment is coming from. That is exactly when you are being given the opportunity to go deep and look and release.

There is something in your ego that is calling your attention. It is asking you not to look at it because it wants to stay! At first, you must be very conscious of how you do this. You will move through this most quickly, you are divinely supported.

SRK: It's also so simple how in the experience of the discomfort of the release that my ego would assume that there was something wrong with me.

Of course! Your ego wants you! You are filled with the energy of the divine at a time of great joy and fulfillment and your ego is strong. You know this. It is a habit! Know that you are full and whole. You are filled with the divine, and you are a carrier of great joy.

Feel at this moment who you truly are. Remember who you are with great joy! Release this ego of illusion that wants you to be in pain…how silly! The greater you embrace your joy, the simpler and easier this mission becomes for you. For you release, and it is done. You carry on with great smiles and great happiness.

Do you feel the difference in your body now?

SRK: Yes, I do! Must the knowing permeate every cell? My old friend the ego, wants to know how to integrate.

What is there to integrate? Your old friend will simply do anything to trick you into staying. Sometimes it is best to love your friends from afar. Thank them for serving you so well.

SRK: I understand.

Imagine the stronger love of your "self," the pure love that you are. Fill yourself with the divine light of love, with the connection with the Elohim that you know so beautifully. Breathe in the peace and the purity that you are, and then the clarity that you so seek shall be apparent. For you cannot force it, it simply is.

This discussion of the ego is very powerful. It is one that I did not fully comprehend in one sitting. The ego holds separation in place by investing in authorities outside of the soul and the connection to God. This I understood. But I did not consider that acts of compassion could also perpetuate separation, and thus perpetuate pain.

Compassion is an expression of love. However, compassion that is rooted in feelings of pain or a desire to make things right will perpetuate the illusion. This is the pain of the pain, which continues to inflame the wound of separation. Actions rooted in anything less than Joy create ripples of separation and ultimately pain. For those actions give power to the perceived enemy.

Once one sees, feels and knows the perfection of all creation, then every act becomes an act of compassion.

We do not have to wait for Enlightenment. When we act from the energy of Joy, our decisions and actions create the conditions from which effective solutions can be birthed. We actually create a new expression from which new possibilities arise. We will never create peace by waging war, we will never end suffering by simply treating the symptom. None of the world's perennial problems were created due to Joy! We must create the conditions from which a different reality can emerge. The solutions to the word's problems will come from a new level of consciousness. We do not need the answer, we only need to create the new field of being. We create a new soil and the flower will naturally bloom. This new soil is the energy of Joy.

Joy is a choice. It emerges naturally from your Authentic Self. And you can accelerate the emergence of your authenticity simply by practicing Joy! Most of us have not yet learned how to sustain Joy because we slip into an ego-induced trance, feel some pain and then began chasing the pain, looking for solutions. Joy transcends the illusions of the ego and thus transcends the problems. Joy is not the solution to a practical problem; it is the energy from which a solution can be birthed.

One day Kiel raised his voice for emphasis and said to me:

If it does not look like joy, why are you doing it?
Sri Ram Kaa, write that down on a piece of paper and look at it throughout the day.

It was then I realized that I had the habit of making things harder and more serious, than they needed to be! Right then I decided that everything, yes everything, I chose to do would be done with Joy or I simply would not do it. What a relief! I had a simple barometer. If I was not feeling Joy in an activity, then either I had succumbed to an ego-trance or I was doing something that was not appropriate for me to do.

Freedom can be yours simply by asking yourself that same question:

"If it does not look like joy, why am I doing it?"

6

Trust, Love and the False Gods

Creator, Let me feel you. Let me know your love...
This day I choose to trust more fully,
to set aside my need to control and simply trust Your hand.
You are in charge of the outcome, dear Lord,
I need only show up and make myself available.

Thank You, God, for letting life flow with such ease.
Thank you, God, for allowing me the exquisite pleasure of being
at the forefront of your unfolding creation.
I am truly grateful.

Sri Ram Kaa's prayer

"Of all the false gods, the body is the greatest illusion."
—Archangel Zadkiel

As we practiced the choice of Joy and the focus on gratitude, the grip of the ego lessened.

Gratitude is the natural state of an open heart. It is simple openness, a simple noticing of the flow that is always there. The heart leads, it sets direction, the mind generates the how. The heart asks for beauty, while the mind asks for answers. Through the focus on gratitude, our minds became quieter. Life simply offered up whatever we needed. Worry or preoccupation did not improve the odds of success. The greater the trust, the greater the gratitude, the greater the flow of abundance.

To spend less time preoccupied with comparison, judgment and the internal pressure to do as others expect, was liberating! We were prepared to move forward with Kiel, and the discourses were becoming ever more powerful, ever more expansive. Occasionally, fear or resistance would surface. It seemed apparent that releasing the ego was a bit like washing water color out of a rag—it took lots of squeezing and rinsing, but it did finally come out.

※

There is a misinterpretation of "Thou shall not put others before me." Are you familiar with this phrase?

SRK: Yes, from the Christian Bible.

That is correct. However, it has a debated background that has been misinterpreted also. Understand this: Anyone who celebrates faith as given by others outside of the authentic self, have put the false Gods in front of them.

You have made Time your God.
You have made Money your God.
You have made Food your God.
And you have made Power your God.

These are the false gods that are on the planet at this time that are causing the great destruction. It is those four.

SRK: That commandment: "Thou shalt have no other gods before me"…is that wisdom in all other religious texts as well?

It is, in different words. Yes, the concept is to just truly be in love and service to the Higher. The word "Higher" is simply given because in your limited definition that was the word that served. Yet the sadness of the word, Higher self or Higher being, creates the illusion of lower. This is how that illusion got started. It was only because of the limited vocabulary and understanding of the interpretation that the word "Higher" was given. There is no Higher Self. There is the Self.

SRK: There is no Higher Self?

No! There is the Self! The Authenticity! It should be the Authentic Self, not the Higher Self. That way we would have the Lower Self. This is very funny to us. Higher! Lower! Greater! Lesser! ... This is very funny!

SRK: If we have no higher or lower then how can we have authentic or inauthentic?

You have the vessel and you have the energy. It is that simple.

What are you feeling, Sri Ram Kaa?

SRK: A release, various releases. My body is purging energies, patterns, releasing fears. In the process of becoming my Self, I am releasing what is not myself. I discovered last night that I have been holding on to things that I was afraid to feel, afraid to resolve.

We ask you these questions because of the truly human evolution you are going through. What you are feeling now must be expressed! Your shift is truly occurring.

SRK: I have been experiencing what I would have called sickness.

Yes, simply the release of the toxins that have held you back. For how else does the vessel know how to release them except through what you call the sickness? All sickness, all sickness, Sri Ram Kaa, is a cry for connection. All sickness. You live in a society that has made a god out of sickness.

SRK: We have made doctors our priests in some ways.

Yes. All sickness is cry for connection. This is important. It is the lack of connection that allows the vessel to be open to receive the sickness. We discuss it because the events that are coming will attack many on the level of sickness and the greater the disconnection the greater the sickness. Your vessel was not designed to be sick and you were placed on a sphere that had everything needed in its fullness to remedy any sickness.

The manifestation of the pharmaceutical application in the treatment of the sick creates more sick, simply because it is not a treatment in the wholeness. It is simply the treatment of the symptom, therefore creating other symptoms.

This has become very manifest in the current society and is also a way by which control can be even more effective. It isolates an entire part of the population that you refer to as "old," by creating a dependency both in the mind and in the body...therefore further removing the connection to the Divine and it becomes almost impossible for those of the old to then reconnect.

For they [the aged], are totally influenced by everything around them.

SRK: Like children.

Yes. This is a great crime. For the purpose of the use of the aging of the body with the wisdom, was protection. It was not to lose the ability to "use" the vessel.

It was not to lose the ability to use the mind. Pay attention, I say "use." Remember, the authentic use of the mind and the body is to serve you. So it was the wisdom and the reconnection that was the purpose of the evolvement of the body to be able to continue the teaching cycle of the young. The teaching cycle was interrupted and turned over to the power of the land to make the decision of the dissemination of what is best. These things started the disconnection of the self-responsibility. How can you ever reconnect if you do not have responsibility for all that you do?

The more that we give away our responsibility and our responsibility for what we do, the greater we disconnect again. Do you see, Sri Ram Kaa, how many ways and enticements are there to take us away from ourselves?

SRK: Bit by bit, step by step.

Yes. It is intricately woven like a fine tapestry that I look at and enjoy. And so it is important to instruct how to maintain the wholeness without the pharmaceuticals. You, yourself, Sri Ram Kaa take too many pharmaceuticals for your stomach. Your stomach calls to you because your solar plexus still carries some constraint and so simply allow the nourishment that you put into your vessel to provide you with the strength to move through this [constraint], and release.

Sri Ram Kaa continues:

This discourse on wholeness and protecting the self was so illuminating and so freeing. Kiel had clearly stated: *All disease is a call for Connection. All disease is a separation.*

In my healing practice, I had witnessed the truth of this. Clients who developed a deeper communication with their body and soul became more peaceful and recovered more quickly. Medical interventions and surgeries save lives, but they really just buy time. They buy time for the patient to become more authentic, more peaceful, ever more healthy. If the patient chooses to wisely use his time to shift preoccupations and create even more joy (this usually looks like a lifestyle change), then the individual evolves into an authentic expression. If no learning comes from the occurrence of the disease, and the pre-disease status quo is maintained, then chances are there will be another illness later in life.

Similarly, emotional discomfort seems to have a progression. If a person does not develop greater emotional flexibility (acceptance of self and others) over time, then chances are there will be little inner peace and serenity in old age. One's outlook on life will become more conservative and fearful and one's circle of friends will become more and more homogeneous. Change will be threatening. As we grow, we are called to widen our circle of love, to expand our sense of family.

Cultivating your inner guidance takes practice. Can you discern the difference between the subtle messages of your soul versus the yearnings of your ego? We are not readily trained to do this. Our culture teaches us to be dependent on outside authorities. Our family of origin, schools, and television all program our value system and expectations. As we have lost touch with true guidance, we have lost touch with true Joy.

Navigating this lesson, we learned that as with other lessons, there are layers to move through. It is important to be evermore accepting of ourselves, to simply be kind to self and others as we explore our experience.

SRK: I am prepared to talk about love now, to listen.

Let us talk about love. This is a subject that I ask only one thing, for you to be totally open and to release as much as possible of your preconception of what love is. You live in a time when love is judgment and where love has also become a false god. The definition of love has changed into a twisted misperception. It is used carelessly and often: I love that thing; I love money.

This is not the essence of love. This type of expression further removes you from the connection and from being able to come home. For as this misconception of love has grown, so has the destruction.

You live in a society that worships children and, yet, simultaneously perverts them in many ways. The entire society is permeated by this distortion, which is evidenced by the display of unhealthy and shadowed paradigms of both the masculine and the feminine.

It is sad to see that the more we worship this false god, love, the more we are so easy to use and to throw the word around without true meaning, the greater the disconnection from true love. At this level, love now has the component of judgment.

I love you, if,
I love you, only,
I love you, maybe,
I love you for a year and a half, and then I love someone else.

When we show this disrespect to the love, we are disrespecting the divine.

There will be those who say, "Oh yes, but you get into a marriage, it is a bad marriage, it is abusive, what is this!" Know that it was never a marriage for it was not based upon divine love. Of course it will be dissolved, for it was never real to begin with. It was part of the illusion of the destruction of the love.

Completely love and respect the divine love that you are!

From your own inside, understand that it was with great love that the vessels were created, that you were provided with all that you needed to sustain yourselves in great joy on this planet. These vessels are gifts, which is why any form of self-mutilation is totally against the god within. When you are totally disconnected from this divine love, that is what it is truly like to be insane.

The search is so hard and long and painful because most do not know what they are looking for, and they have greater illusion of society telling them that it is selfish to love within, that they should feel guilty to love within, that it is a sin to love within.

These messages serve only the dark, because when we do not love within, we are unable to move forward in any direction. We cause a cycle of pain and joy, pain and joy, because we are not living our fullness.

How could anyone enter into a relationship for a long term if they have first not yet reconnected with the absolute, for then the relationship becomes the reflection of the absolute, and the love is not even a question, it is simply there. You can feel it in the heart of the one next to you. You can see it in their eyes. You know the power of the energy that surrounds you. There is richness and a fullness that cannot be found in the shallowness. Love is truly what binds our soul together.

The soul has much love as a component, and so I must address for you the love and how to relax into this love. Without the true relaxing, love cannot be. So, the relaxing into love is about the unconditional love within yourself, loving every part of yourself that you may not love now. Blessing God for the opportunity just to be here, to be able to look at this opportunity.

Wholeness is your birthright, and if wholeness is your birthright, than so is love. Whatever is your birthright shall come forth, for of course it never left, it was simply twisted and challenged.

Remember that when you are in wholeness, it is your authentic self that is guiding. For you are no longer clinging to the illusion, and you are no longer living in the false god of love.

We had now been acquainted with two very powerful false gods, the body and love. This concept of misplaced worship was so close, and yet, we were hungry for evermore illumination. Were there more false gods? Of course!

On this planet you have a saying, "In the beginning of time." Throughout the cultivation of society there has been a need to disconnect from the natural flow of the earth. For as we sit here you notice that the sun has kept perfect time for us. Yet, when we have forgotten that we trust that the sun will keep the time for us, we then become dependent on the devices.

In the time before the devices and the recognition of what you call time and calendar there was simply the integration of many worlds. For all exist simultaneously...yet independent. Each sphere of energy that has travelers was created to allow for the evolution and expansion of love.

In the beginning simply means when you are still connected, when you still have conscious memory that you are a traveler on the path of evolution.

Known as the pure ones, the light that emanated from this planet was so bright that it attracted all. In the attraction, where the light is so brilliant, there must also be dark. And so, the dark was integrated so that all was in harmony.

It has been the misaligning of the masculine/feminine balance which has led to the escalation of the power-oriented humanity. Power is another false god, which we will discuss later.

There have been many misconceptions that come in with the power oriented energy. The first was "time." For the concept of the second, the minute, the hour, the time and the calendar were to put limits on that which you can connect with. The adherence to this allows one to increase their judgment, therefore increasing the separation.

For with the acceptance of time and the belief in this system, one has judgment about the perception of completion. One then believes in aging, one believes in death, one believes in the concept of control, one believes in all matters in regards to finality. For they all end at a specific time and they all begin at a specific time, which in and of itself was a creation not of the Elohim.

In your modern world, time has become a god. It is the ultimate disconnection.

Instead of worshipping and honoring with gratitude the love and the creation and the mystery of this beautiful experience, one chooses to worship, if they have enough time. It has become a deity. Monuments are built to it. It is made ever more precise. And it is a status symbol.

For the greater your power, the greater your symbol of disconnection that you wear on your body like a prize and an honor. It marks events in your life and it ticks on slowly like a meter of death robbing you of joy. This is how we perceive linear time as it has come to be demonstrated here.

SRK: So linear time became necessary to create discernment?

Separation!

SRK: But what came first?

The linear time I refer to is the twelve o'clock, one o'clock calendar. So it was the creation of the ever-increasing power energy of the planet.

SRK: To control events?

Correct. In order to put a finality on events. It is a control mechanism; it is a way of ruling. For everything is judged by that and with that judgment it finds more judgment. All judgment becomes predicated and when we enter this planet we are immediately given the time!

There is a time when we are born.
There is a time that we die.
There is a time that we eat. We are told, "It is time!"
There is a time we go to school. We are told "It is time!"

It has removed all personal responsibility and development. Some are meant to increase their time. Some are meant to go to schooling at different times, some are meant to do things at different times, yet the "time" does not allow this, because the definition of time is to limit. It is to disconnect from the Joyous Creator. It is to rob you of that which naturally will evolve for you.

The only time that should matter is that of the highest energy of the sun, which is at the sunrise and the sunset. For all that marks is the time of the shift of the energy. There is one energy that is pervasive in your body, as you know it on this planet, when the sun is up, and there is a different energy that is in your body that is pervasive on this planet when the sun is down.

It is the balance of the sun up and the sun down that creates perfect harmony, and it is all you need to know. For we play tricks in the great society of our time. We change our time at will. We go back and forth in time at will. Even now you have a time machine on this planet you call a "plane."

SRK: An airplane?

Yes, for you can be in a different time very quickly. It is crude, a beginning. Time exists only in the balance of the light and the dark. Wearing time as a monument on the body injures your energy field. You should refrain from wearing all time on your body.

SRK: You mean timepieces?

Yes. For the energy disrupts the meridian conduit and all attempts to reconnect it will disharmonize once the time is put back on the body. The only way to start breaking the chain is to remove yourself from the time that is the concept on this planet. For when you do so you will immediately notice the habit of being controlled by this. You will know that it is no longer serving you to be controlled by this.

When you are able to discern things by the amount of light needed to accomplish them, then, you can use the sun, or lack of sun, effectively. Embodying this concept means that you must truly release the concept that is misunderstood on this planet of the breakfast, and the lunch, and the dinner, and the sleep, and the wake time. This cannot be easily done in the society, and yet it must be.

It is important to honor the cycle within you, and to honor that all cycles are different. Yet, when groups of like-minded individuals are able to be together, their energy resonates as with the tribes not yet touched by civilization. They do have a time structure, yet they are not bound by this other than how their bodies and their tribe has survived in the most beneficial manner in honor of their commitment to connection. Their commitment to the use of light, the sun.

Of course I am speaking of those who are not touched by the society now but those who are living free from the constraining and the control of time.

We are instinctual as a race on this planet. You move away from your instincts in many forms and time does this for you. You may wish to experiment with the removal of all time until you are comfortable with no longer letting it control you. Yet, you must also not try to control it.

It is the first and most important step in embracing the true connection. From it you can truly learn to release the judgment, the self-inflicted pressure of accomplishment on a certain frame of time. If one was to remove all of these perceived time constraints, the freed energy available to your evolution would be amazing and provide the opportunity to move into greater union with the Creator in a much faster way.

It is important to know that time has no relevance at home for you. The release is so important now. The concept of "time" at home is like folding time which is very different than the controlled time that we are speaking of on this planet.

SRK: Folding time as opposed to controlled time?

Correct. There truly is no beginning and no end. The need to find a "big bang" is very funny. There is no "big bang." There is Expansion.

To remove the control of the time, one must surrender unconditionally. This is a challenge. It is accomplished by simply focusing on the love that is within and without, and around. For then the connection of love and time as you know it becomes *irrelevant. You realize that there is always time. You release that the illusion of the beginning and the end is also part of the evolution of the soul.*

When you are finally able to break through the illusion you find the bliss, and you find the abundance. You find the joy and you find the Beloved. It is at that time that you know there is no time. And the acceptance of the One is simply natural.

There need not be a question, for even the question feels like a place in time. There will be much more to learn about time in the next book. Yet, in this book it is important to know about the elimination of the honoring of the time on the wrist.

Kiel talks of the fact that we have paced our lives around time. His discourse seems simple, yet we wish to point out the power of what is being communicated. Culturally, we have divided up our lives into segments. For example, there is awaking time, breakfast time, school starting time, time to go to work, lunch time, and commuting time. This segmentation is taken for granted. However, the effect of this artificial structure is to separate us from our natural rhythms. Energy flows through us in cycles that are similar, yet unique, for each individual.

The time segments offer mechanisms of control. These controls are as simple as programming our appetites to match the standard meal times and regulating the flow of factory production. The result is that the daylight hours are spent indoors for most people and that society in general conforms to a fairly standardized routine.

Routine offers predictability and control. Routine can also be reassuring. But this reassurance is the peace *of the ego.* Is not an external routine little more than a substitute for inner reliance? Is not an external routine a dependency upon something other than self? This is the essence of Kiel's message. We have surrendered the authority for our comings and goings to people and conventions outside of ourselves. We have stopped attending to our inner voices and simply fallen into automatic patterns. We have done so willingly, eagerly, and unconsciously. The result is further surrender to the ego, and ever more separation from the Divine.

Kira Raa shares:

When I first removed my watch in April, 2002, I felt somehow naked and lost. For days I would absent-mindedly look at my wrist. Often, I would find myself panic-stricken over wanting to know the time. It was a startling reality to note how dependent I had been to my *time god*. It took me ten months to stop routinely looking at my wrist for the answer.

During that same ten months, however, I began to notice my body's natural rhythms. The release of the time was another powerful lesson that further opened the door to my Authenticity and the Self-Ascension process.

There are many other false Gods. The God of money. This is another false God. Power is a false God.

SRK: Yes, I see that power can be in business, politics, or…

Anything that creates control over you or others. Many get drunk with power.

In the world of the ego, the goals of the game are designed to stimulate passion for the illusion. Thus, power or its consort, money, are ever-popularized as goals. Neither power nor money is intrinsically unhealthy. However, the drive for these goals strengthens separation consciousness. That drive is rooted in fear. Many who sought money or power discover that they are devoid of true satisfaction. This is an important learning. Some learn by pursuing the experience, others learn by looking deeply. Both ways are appropriate.

It really boils down to two points of view: Trust or Fear. If you develop your spiritual awareness, you are naturally led to the truth that the universe is in a state of perfection; Love is everywhere. If you place your attention on the world of the ego, then you will uncover more and more evidence of separation, lack, and reasons to be fearful.

Power, as it is commonly understood, comes from an assumption that something is lacking. What follows is a belief that the lack can be resolved by exercising control over something or somebody. All forms of control come from a lack of trust. That lack of trust is really a disconnection from God.

The pathway Home is paved with devotion, surrender and trust. At some point along this path, one comes to the understanding that true Power is alignment with Truth. It is the expression of the fullness of God. Thus, the power we truly seek is communion with God. From that communion, wisdom and beauty flow like a stream from the mountain. This state of communion aligns us with the authentic flow. This spiritual power often resides with the elders, the wise ones, the ones who offer counsel not control. So I ask: Where are the elders? Where are those in our community that support the rituals of transition? Where are the wisdom-keepers, the white-haired men, the crones?

Kiel challenges us to be response-able, to dive with love back into the Self that we are by simply walking into our Authenticity. To simply say "thank you" to the Divine, and an opportunity to further heal the separation, to re-claim our true power, and remember love.

The elders, the white-haired men, the crones, the holders of the ritual, they all exist. They are you, they are me, they are us.

Section Three
Unconditional Love

Fearing the "fall"
Of falling in love,
I clung to the ego's walls…

Let go! Let go! Let go!

Dive into that sea,
Let the sea become you
And you are free!

Let your soul lead
Let your precious soul
Have the reins.

Be fully present
To the unfolding chaos
And the order
Reveals itself.

Sri Ram Kaa

7

Authentic Soul Nourishment

Eat only whole grains, fruit, vegetables, and no eggs.

❦

This was only the beginning.

❦

Kira Raa shares:

When Sri Ram Kaa and I were first given these simple eating instructions we were in the middle of the desert, in a self-contained rental RV, and our refrigerator was packed with all our favorite foods. Our camping food included a lot of plastic-wrapped goodies! We had even brought along an espresso maker! And, by the way, *nothing from the cow.*

What! What about my morning latte? And just what is so bad about a veggie omelet? What about the Brie in the refrigerator? For that matter, what about the yogurt, the pudding, and the ice cream! *Who was this "Kiel guy" and why was he torturing me?*

Prior to this trip, I had been secretly yearning to lose that extra weight. After all, the desert meant scanty clothing. So, even though I protested losing my favorite foods, part of me reasoned that giving up my beloved cheese and milk products certainly would not harm my figure.

I had been riding the body shame cycle my whole life! It was time to get real with myself and to finally get happy with my body. After all, it had lovingly supported me for 42 years! Perhaps it was time for me to accept who I was. *Who was I kidding?*

Over the years, the depth of my eating disorders—binge, purge, lose, gain—had become deeply entrenched in the "who" that I thought I was. I pretended that I was Okay with my body but I carried tons of self-judgment. *Calm down,* I said to myself, searching for reassurance. *Don't show Sri Ram Kaa your alarm. Now you have a spiritual reason for a food plan. Try this diet for a few days. Breathe.*

Had I known what Sri Ram Kaa was thinking and feeling about my body, I would have been devastated. What made it worse was that *I did* sense his disapproval. He *did* have negative judgments about my body. I was in denial. I tried my best to take the high road. The *it's his stuff* affirmation was running at warp speed in my head; it was chased by the phrase *just get over it.*

How could I be in love with someone who was so judgmental of my body? How could I, indeed! Sure, *he* had no idea what having a baby at 39 does to a woman. Was he unaware of how much pain I was in? After all, he was not exactly the picture of fitness. Why the double standard, and worse, why was I unbothered by his imperfections?

This was a too-familiar self-depreciating loop that had no place in my life. It was my time to sincerely look at it, and to heal it.

Sri Ram Kaa was open and honest about his inner battle to release his own judgments about my body. The gift of his honesty and our shared value about being transparent with our communication, led me to realize that I could never love myself while I too was so judgmental of my body.

The time had come to simply nourish myself and release the outcome. I decided to no longer pay attention to calories; I would eat that which truly nourished my soul and my body. I simply followed the food recommendations provided to us by Zadkiel. It wasn't about my size. It wasn't about my body. It was about connection. It was about authenticity. It was about a commitment to Self-Ascension.

What began as a simple three day program has now become a lifestyle. Amazingly, I no longer crave that which does not nourish me, and I know the difference. Zadkiel explained that the nourishment program is much more than simply a food regime; it is a lifestyle that properly nourishes the soul as well as the body. A pattern of living I now chose with joy, and share with gratitude.

The nourishment program is not just about food. It is also about fresh air, sunshine, pure water and staying connected with your

Beloved. I *know* what it has done and continues to do for me. I am off the harsh anti-depressants. I am off the constant self-bashing. I am nourished with love and I know that it begins and stays with me.

I am truly happy, and I am truly at peace. When I find myself off-center, it now only takes moments to step back into the clarity of Joy. I thought this state of being was impossible for me. I never dreamed that I would one day embody these qualities. It was actually simple. After sticking out my foot, taking a step, and walking through the fear, my authenticity began to shine through!

As with most couples, we had similar yet different experiences as we embarked on our nourishment adventure. Here is Sri Ram Kaa's experience.

❦

Sri Ram Kaa shares:

Denial is the classic double standard. We avoid noticing our own shortcomings by projecting our flaw on another. I had been living the spiritual high road. I knew that God was in everything. I knew that the role of a mate is to deepen our ability to love. I knew that I should look at my Beloved and see the Goddess.

Well, I discovered that the Goddess had cellulite! I have learned that the Goddess had irregular teeth and did not fit into a size four! I discovered that the Goddess sometimes made snoring sounds when sleeping. *How can this be?* How dare she fall short of the Yoga-perfect, New Age Madison Avenue Goddess!

Observing my inner thoughts, it became painfully obvious to me that I had unconsciously adopted a superficial standard for beauty. I was attracted to thin, athletic women. If the candidate female met this standard, then I would look deeper for the God-essence. That is, if the person didn't meet my beauty standards, I wouldn't bother considering them as a potential mate.

What part of me wanted to be pleased by this beauty stereotype? It was the part of me that wanted other men to nod with approval, that wanted my partner to gain me social points, and the part of me that believed there existed some sort of external approval scale. I feared being laughed at. When I followed my feelings to their source, I actually heard my mother's voice condemning *fat women.* Was I still wanting my mother's approval?

All of these Parts were viewpoints of the ego. All were created as false antidotes to fear, especially the fear of others' opinions. I had just received a good dose of reality therapy, and it had a name: Kira Raa. And here I was, projecting my unfinished business on Kira again. Was Kira fat? No, she was not. I had already gone through this in Sedona. A month later judgments again contaminated our joy. I had set aside these thoughts before. I knew that to find peace I must learn how to permanently move past these judgments. But how could I do that?

Healing requires that we love the disowned parts of ourselves. In the Sacred Union, the potential for healing is far greater than any other venue, for the love of the Beloved rapidly dissolves fear. However, in order to arrive there, one must first bring the disowned parts of self into the relationship. There can be no more running away, no more pretending, no more withholding. I needed to allow the icky, sticky, grumpy, and scary parts to come to the surface. In the Sacred Union, they *will* surface. One does not need to go fishing for them; they automatically arise. The trick is to remember that the goal is freedom from fear. That means doing the opposite of what the ego would have one do, for stepping through fear dissolves fear. One must suspend judgment and trust that the love of the Union will heal the wounds. When one partner holds the energy of love for the other partner, miracles happen. Love heals.

All judgment serves to separate us from the exquisite joy of creation. All judgment is a form of separation and it wounds. All separation generates pain. It *is* that simple. Pain or Joy; separation or oneness. Choose! No therapist can ever bring the depth of resolution to you that your Beloved can bring. The Sacred Union can heal anything. Anything can be healed, for in the Sacred Union is the energy of God. Love heals.

No one voluntarily chooses to feel pain. As I brought my attention to my inner space, I felt the pain of my struggle to stay in control. I felt the grief of separation, the many years that I had focused on outward beauty to compensate for my own fear that I would be ridiculed. To protect me from my fear that *I was not good enough,* my ego had me focus on the outer world. The pain had nothing to do with anyone outside of me—I had never truly learned how to surrender, for it is in the surrender that we discover our divinity. In spite of my deep faith in God, I had not yet taken this final step. I was still wanting to control the outer world and thus not have to confront my inner secrets.

Kira's presence gave me the opportunity to deeply feel the price of ego control. No one told me to let go and surrender. Yet, I could feel the agony of my habit. I felt the fear and the isolation that accompanies the need to control. Who was really in charge here, my personality-self or my soul? Let the soul lead!

Until this relationship I did not understand that true Union with your partner meant union with Self. I was frightened of my own criticism. I was scared to feel my fear, yet once I did feel it, I experienced greater self-acceptance and then the judgments stopped. True Union means bringing the light of unconditional love to your partner and to yourself. It is the ultimate surrender, as all judgment must be suspended and the energy of unconditional love brought to the forefront. When self-judgment is suspended, the disowned aspects of self come forward for healing.

The healing was not instantaneous. What was required was that each time either one of us felt shame, fear or pain, we were called to share it and to be transparent. This brings the light of Love to the negative beliefs and feelings. The process of Self-Ascension requires that anything that is unlike love be dissolved. How can you heal if you refuse to accept a part of yourself? How can you be an instrument for pure love if you have any doubt or shame left? These feelings are indications of inner separation and must be healed in order to experience Union. Over a period of three months, trusting the love of the Union, we brought much of what was hidden into the Light.

Through the process of surrendering to the love of the Union, we dissolved the intricacies of our own egos and brought ever more love into our day-to-day experience. All that was required was trust. Our souls brought the fire of purification to us. Each time a negative thought or feeling arose we were at a choice point: avoid it or heal it. Love worked its way into every shadow bringing the light of liberation to our experience.

One day Kiel offered the following steps for Self-Ascension through the Sacred Union.

1. *Be in Union*
2. *Suspend judgment*
3. *Surrender*
4. *Unconditional Love*

These four steps are simple and powerful. They will dissolve the grip of the ego on your experience. To be in Union requires that one doesn't run away or keep secrets. If you are withholding something then your pain is doubled for not only are you holding on to the pain of your inner experience but you are also experiencing the pain of separation from your Beloved. To suspend judgment is simply a decision to be present to the process of the moment, to set aside your evaluations. To surrender is to release the need to control. This allows the flow of Love to work its way into the situation. The experience of unconditional love is the result of trust. It begins with acceptance and the knowing that all is of God and all is therefore perfect. Any time you feel pain, that is, something other than Peace or Joy, it is a reminder to step into the model. Follow the four steps. Your liberation awaits!

The delight of the release of the ego!

The true rapture of releasing the burden of the body, floating ever lighter!

For you are now beginning to see the power of the food that you are taking in, in combination with the vibrational shifts that are occurring.

SRK: I am beginning to know, I have not yet seen. (Laughing)

That is fine, so we propose this question for you to ponder: Is it truly bliss to eat that which may taste appealing to the body and yet leave you feeling afterwards sad and confused, or up, only to come down?

Or, is it bliss to consume that which you know is nourishing you and further, allows you to be in constant Peace and Joy? Which is truly satisfying?

And so, before you ingest, you simply say, "Which am I serving, my bliss of authenticity or my pallet? Which will enhance all aspects of that which I am? How do I nourish myself?"

Replace the word eating with nourishing. This is an important distinction. We do not eat. For in the belief system that we eat, it has allowed the perversion of many attractive food preparations that do not serve. When we nourish we recognize the true meaning of sustenance for this body and everything will change. It is not "time" to eat, it is "time" to nourish.

SRK: As I was preparing my breakfast this morning I noticed that what I ate did not seem to fully satisfy me. I wonder: Does the soul know all with respect to the physical world...what substances and chemicals in this world would be offensive or nourishing to the vessel?

No, the soul in and of itself has no knowledge of this world. That is why the soul comes into a vessel. When the soul comes into a vessel, the integration requires several things. The first is that the soul loses all conscious memory of the authenticity. The second is the soul agrees to exist based upon the needs of the vessel.

You first have this agreement to live by the requirements of the vessel. The vessel initially dictates its wants and needs based upon how you are raised by your parents or whoever is feeding you. You do not have much conscious choice for many years.

You simply have things put in front of you. As you are learning to nourish, is that not a physical manifestation of the same type of the agreement that the soul made to forget its authenticity? For you have also relinquished control of that which is nourishing you and are at the subject of those you had chosen to do this for you. It is a small model of what is to come.

For as you grow, you make your own choices on nourishment usually based upon that which provides you gratification in terms of taste and sensation. This is why the younger you are the choices are more based upon instant satisfaction on only the level of the physical. For the awareness is not yet present. Is this not a beautiful physical manifestation of what is happening with your authenticity?

So as you keep growing, you start receiving other information that may or may not be consistent with the information you have already been given regarding nourishment. Some are provided all prepared food and they feel very drawn toward prepared food and their information has been that everything comes in as a prepared process. Others, not many, but others, have been raised on the concept of fresh food and nutrition and energy. This group is growing.

Yet when I speak with you, I speak of a time when you were raised that it was the meat and potatoes. And so you have had to explore and allow yourself to break through belief systems to find those foods that serve your soul. While your body, or your vessel, still craves that which it wants.

This has nothing to do with what you want.

For as you have grown you have become greater in the understanding of who you really is. The vessel serves you. Yet that is also an evolutionary process. You are not born knowing this. And you are conditioned away from it and must also return home to it. And so when you say that you were not satisfied with your breakfast, what were you looking for? Was it you that was not satisfied, or was it your vessel? You are learning the difference.

This is part of the discernment that can only come in as you release the ego. You are creative. You are growing. Perhaps it is time to start researching and looking for ways to be served that would satisfy you nutritionally in the framework of the food that will support your vibrational level. You are fortunate to live at a time and in a place where these are readily available.

SRK: Yes. So that leads to the question hidden within this question: Do people damage their vessels through ignorance?

Yes. And through the length of the dis—connection with their authenticity

SRK: So does the soul know? Does the authentic soul know?

The soul only knows how to evolve and expand. Listen to the answers. Keep it simple, Sri Ram Kaa.

SRK: Thank you! If I have a cup of poison in front of me what keeps me from ingesting it?

Nothing if your vessel is in control and your ego is in control, nothing. If your authentic self is present, then you must deeply go into your authentic self and communicate with your vessel to receive your answer. The soul knows through the vessel.

SRK: Aha! Yes! Because my experience has been that I know much about things I know nothing about…through the muscle testing[8] and inquiry.

Correct. And we are saying the same thing with different words. This is good exercise. This is the proper union of the soul and the vessel because it is the authentic soul that is working with the vessel.

SRK: There is a dialog and exchange of information. The vessel knows the material world, the soul knows the direction…

Yes. The question is: who is making the decision? That is the question.

SRK: So this little testing I do, muscle testing, is a technique from Kinesiology for testing for herbs, for testing the wisdom of the body. I see no error in this.

No, there is none.

SRK: Except for myself I realize that it is still an externalization as opposed to just simply knowing.

That is correct. For there is no error in this other than it is a means for those who are still growing. You will find that you will no longer need it. You no longer need it now, if you walk into trust for is not the testing a way of double-checking your own trust?

SRK: Yes.

How could you ever move completely into trust if you must check everything?

---

[8]Muscle Testing is a technique developed by practitioners of Applied Kinesiology and other professionals to determine whether a substance or thought is in alignment with a person's health or highest wisdom.

SRK: Yes, it is a crutch.

Yes, a dependency. There is much for many to learn around the subject of proper sustenance of the vessel. And the proper sustenance of the vessel was designed in the beginning not to eat any form of flesh. You are not flesh eaters.

SRK: And these teeth?

These teeth did not look like this. They have evolved because of the way that you have evolved in your systems of eating.

SRK: Our science doesn't show that record.

Of course not.

SRK: So, our science then supports the belief system that was already in place.

That is correct. And why would it not? Is not the ego totally influenced by making sure that it protects itself at all costs? So would not therefore the ego go out and seek to prove and find means to prove that which it wants to hold on to?

SRK: Absolutely. I have a few cravings for meat left. I notice sometimes when I have what I interpret as a craving for meat, what I am really wanting is grounding.

That is correct.

SRK: And that grounding I seek is actually a centering in self, so to speak, but I am still in the habit of externalizing, of thinking I need something from the outside.

Bear in mind that the ego will translate that into meat because the more meat you ingest, the heavier your vibration and the more inability to connect with authenticity. This inability to connect with authenticity has become such a large means of control that it has led to imbalance on the planet. It has led to influence your political systems globally and it is means of control for many. It is a means of livelihood for many and It is out of control. It is part of why the planet must evolve. For the eating of meat causes de-evolution. And gross over-breeding of many animals that has caused great waste on the planet causing much pollution, causing much destruction of necessary oxygen-producing plants and life sustaining systems are being damaged.

SRK: True sustenance for the body is sustenance that brings ever more joy into the body.

Correct, and so it must not cause any pain. Many people suffer from gastric distress; many suffer disorders of the body. All of this is related to the fact that they are eating, not nourishing. This is a pervasive belief system, especially in the country where you sit now, for there has been a great misconception of the true nourishment of the body.

SRK: Yet, how can one step into the recognition of true nourishment when one is invested in fear and separation? Because true nourishment is a harmony, is a joyful union, and *eating* is merely an expression of the separation, of the need for grounding into wholeness.

Have you not answered your own question? Let us recap for you. Have you not yourself been going through this evolutionary process?

SRK: Indeed, but what is pulling me through the forest of illusion is my soul's urging, my desire for the union, the taste of the divine that has been given, that I've known…do *all* have that?

Yes! Of course! All six billion have! It is simply a question of their choice of activation and how this will occur. It is simply an evolutionary process to recognize the distinction between eating and nourishing, as it has been for you. You have escalated your vibratory energy as your nourishment has been changing. You do not need the levels and quantities of nourishment that have been previously your history.

SRK: Is this recognition a symbolic act?

It is both symbolic and it is necessary on a cellular level of the vessel.

SRK: There are many that chose a, and this is an old word, diet, in order to achieve a result, and what we are living is a diet in order to sustain a being.

Understand that this word, "diet," is very important not to use, or to use with distinctions. Many diet to obtain a result of ego-gratification.

SRK: It is to perpetuate separation.

Yes, it is because the body, the appearance of the body is a God in this country in which you reside, and in many other countries around the world. And so they diet to be able to achieve an image that has nothing to do with nourishment. If they happen to achieve by accident some form of improved health, this is considered a benefit, but it is not the primary reason, connection is not the reason.

SRK: So there is only one way through, my being what I truly am. Will others recognize that in themselves?

When the true self appears and when the connection is entered into and is moving toward enhancement and completion, then the subject of how we nourish and how we take in nourishment shifts to simplicity. There will be those who say, "My goodness, how can I not eat my favorite foods? My goodness, does this mean I can never eat this food again?" Is this not ego in the body, is it not?

SRK: Yes.

And so to know that this is truly of a connective path the true will find themselves when reaching out of habit, for that which no longer serves, they will be able to stop by simply remembering that the lack of the ingestion of these foods is a means of honoring the god that they are. A means of honoring the authentic self, of saying I love you, I am taking care of you.

SRK: As an offering.

The release of the so-called favorite foods becomes one of a gift to God.

SRK: This reminds me of how in some monasteries the practice of abstinence from food has been perhaps perverted into an egoic act.

Absolutely, for is it not then simply pain of the pain? My suffering is so great that I must love you [God] so much... No ...Suffering is not a form of love, be clear on that.

SRK: I want to understand this, so what we are offering God is a gift of spaciousness, not a contraction around a favorite food?

Yes, for is not that favorite food a means of disconnect from God?

SRK: Absolutely.

Yes, is it not a disconnect from the love of the self? Find me one person who is suffering with much favorite food that is truly in love with the authenticity of who they are. For those that need to release, are those that have the greatest vibration within them. For this has also been a means of self-medication, all self-medication occurs when the strength of the ego is doing its best to keep you from yourself.

SRK: I am seeing myself in many, many patterns; for example, the emptiness I feel in my stomach, and my habit pattern is to interpret that as a call to go fill up, to become less aware.

Of course, that is why it is there. Perhaps you nourish that emptiness with joy and with sustenance that nourishes the joy. For when we ingest foods simply because the palate claims that it is enjoyable, and then must subsequently provide additional medication to be able to process the food, have we truly nourished? Is it any surprise that as we come closer to the time of great evolutionary joy that so many are experiencing such discomfort in the area of their digestion of foods, and the assimilation of foods?

This is why cancer, this is why disease, this is why mental infirmity. It is all based upon the ingestion based on pleasure, and not nourishment. It is an intricacy woven like a fine tapestry that I look at and enjoy. It is important to maintain wholeness without the pharmaceuticals. Fresh water, good nourishment, love, sacred union with the partner, these will all remove disease from you. It will remove for all who chose this method. Is not this pleasure a choice?

SRK: The pleasure is a substitute for deep trust.

The pleasure is a substitute not only for the deep trust but also a substitute for the joy of the connection of authenticity. So it has been replaced with a superficial joy, many people will say, I "enjoy" eating.

SRK: Right.

Perhaps they can be In-Joy with nourishment rather than to enjoy the eating. Nourishment is a celebration, there is much joy. You may gather with others and be in much joy and give thanks and participate, and through nourishment, be of the highest level.

Tomorrow you begin the 2 days of liquids. It will be most cleansing and beneficial. It would serve you to do this every thirty days. This will be most beneficial. Learn to pay attention to truly what your vessel needs to sustain and heal, rather than what your body is demanding because of habit.

SRK: Yes, thank you. I still carry a touch of confusion around taking good care of the body.

Yes, what is your confusion?

SRK: I have a habit of thinking that foods are required to take care of the body.

They are. It is a question of which foods. There are those that sustain the body, and those that sustain the ego. It is a question of which sustenance you choose to ingest. Yes, these vessels require energy.

SRK: The question answers itself as I reside in my being-ness as opposed to residing in the separation.

Correct. How beautiful a lesson. How beautiful your service that you give so willingly to participate in this evolutionary time by allowing that which you are to experience. That is true compassion. When you allow yourself to experience that which others are experiencing, that is compassion. To be able to embrace it. That is compassion. To understand the Joy, and the Peace and the Love...that is compassion.

Drowning in the sorrow is not compassion, it is perpetuation.

The Elohim came to guide us toward Self-Ascension. The practices are designed to help all experience who they truly are. Training and practice are required.

Without guidance one can become trapped and confused. Hold these practices sacred for it is a path of completion.

Of all the false gods, the body is the greatest illusion.

The nourishment plan is more than a food program: it defines a healthy relationship with the body and with the soul; it helps flush out unconscious ego patterns; it brings one's awareness ever-closer to the Authentic self.

The typical person in western society has lost touch with the authentic hunger of the body. Food has become a method of feeding the ego, medicating the pain of separation, providing entertainment, and supporting the profits of national corporations. If you want to live aligned with your true identity then you will need to discard the illusions that surround food. You can do this gently by realigning your priorities.

This did not happen overnight for us. It was easy to add more fresh produce to our diet. It was less easy to stop eating milk products. We acquired a taste for soy milk. We continued to eat fish three times a week for about six weeks. We still indulged in chocolate and sugared treats for a time. After a month of consistently integrating this form of nourishment, the cravings dramatically subsided. Our bodies simply stopped craving familiar foods. It seemed that the purer we became, the easier it was to select nourishing foods. It was a natural ever more refining cycle. We never experienced dieter's conflict for we were not dieting.

There were habits; like mindlessly consuming a bowl of ice cream or popcorn while watching a video. These cravings were seen for what they truly were, habits. So we would experiment. One evening we would give in to the craving and then see how we felt afterwards. When the craving arose the next evening, we would move closer together and embrace, snuggle and then see how we felt. Guess what? Hugs are more nourishing than any comfort food!

As the days became weeks, it became easy and even humorous to occasionally visit the "old friend" who desired the favorite food, and bless it for the gift of remembrance. We were no longer the victims of habit. We could choose.

***

Pure Foods, Minerals, Air, Sunshine, Keeping the body spotlessly clean. These are all the components of keeping the body functioning at optimum level for you. They are not difficult and you should try to get a little of each every day. Do your best. Fresh air done through walking is very good for the body—even a few minutes. Fresh sunshine—these all activate your cells. Nothing needs to be done excessively...simply in a moderation that recognizes with your soul: "Ahaa, this feels good, yes, I feel nurtured. I feel healthy." This is how it should be done.

Nourishment, as taught by Kiel, is not just about feeding the body. It is about elevating the vitality of the body and the soul. As the soul exists in a synergistic relationship with the body, taking good care of the body should be a joyful undertaking. Walking in nature with the intent to breathe deeply and harmonize with sky, sun and earth is healing for the body and soul. Walking briskly offers aerobic benefits. This is one of the easiest ways to maintain spiritual, emotional and physical health. It is not body-building; it is joyful health maintenance.

Spiritual work is not undertaken at the expense of the body. Nor is maintenance of the vessel performed at the expense of the soul. True cooperation and harmony requires mindfulness and appropriate focus. This is why yoga is an excellent way to maintain health; it combines the spiritual and physical components in a harmonious fashion.

Kiel's message could be rephrased like this: "Simply listen. Listen to the urges of the body, notice the urges of the ego, feel the urges of your soul. Learn to discern the difference. Then choose an action that reflects your commitment to live authentically."

***

One day we realized that we were actually living a vegan lifestyle. We were eating fresh vegetables daily, drinking plenty of pure water, buying only organic produce, and juice fasting two days every month. We had become selective about the restaurants we visited, and yes, we were nourishing at home more often.

There was a great gift in coming home to nourish. Prior to Kiel's influence there often was the dread of cooking, and the "how quick can I microwave" attitude. This attitude has been replaced with the energy of love and gratitude, which permeates all that we ingest. Preparing the food of nourishment is a gift to God, a gift to our authentic being. We send a message of honor and love to our vessel for supporting us. We bless our food before ingesting it and bring the energy of gratitude to every meal.

The body is your servant, not your master. By properly nourishing the vessel, the synergistic relationship between body and soul can flourish. An essential harmony returns and disease, discomfort and dysfunction leave the vessel. As our vitality and Joy increased, we found deep appreciation for learning the difference between nourishing and eating.

Have we given up anything? We have only given up discomfort, illusion, and the false god of food. It was a simple endeavor, one that opened the door to greater visions, higher vibratory levels and deeper connection. In short, we are now nourishing the Joy of authentic living!

*"I believe it to be possible for every human being
to attain that blessed and indescribable state in which
he feels within himself the presence of God."*

—Gandhi

8

Exhaling into Self-Ascension

God, you have gifted us with the spark of eternity. You have allowed us to descend into density to enjoy the experience of rising-up once again. You are the sun in my sky, the life in my blood, the love in my heart. I seek only You, for all else is a temporary pleasure.

God, God, God, let me feel you, let me see your hand in all I behold this day. Let me know your peace. This is my prayer. What I seek today is to know the infinite fullness of Truth…to delight in the paradox of being both human and Divine at the same time. I seek to embrace my humanity without forgetting my Spirit.

I choose to love my foibles…to laugh at my limitations, to chuckle at my ego. Lord, I choose to enjoy this life. I choose to live in joy and bring joy to all I behold. I let this be so now, and so it is!

Prayer of Sri Ram Kaa

The essence of Self-Ascension is the ability to trust so fully that the ego surrenders to God.

***

It is time; it is your time to be home. You must practice daily and, optimally, you should practice twice daily. It does not matter the time. You simply start communicating, so that we may continue to bring you even greater knowledge. It is important that you release all self-imposed constraints of time, all self-imposed constraints of claiming of where to be, what to do, how to do it, because in the surrender, in the allegiance, we honor that in your present state on this planet you must have assistance. We understand.

Each of you radiates at a beautiful level of your own radiation. Feel your energy of who you truly are. Be complete Unconditional Love and Peace. Know who you are and remember who you truly are. Move through the vessel. There are those of you who are light bearers and there are those of you who will need to find a light bearer to complete. It is that simple. There is no hierarchy, there is no higher or lower, there are simply teachers. Much love, great teachers.

We welcome you with the most gratitude and humility. Know that we love you dearly. All we ask is that you love yourself. You must love yourself. You must do everything from a perspective of joy, from love, from a release of judgment. Simply ask yourself, is this truly of the highest service, and does it bring me joy?

For all you need to do is trust the Universe explicitly. For in the Universe, trust and love are one. There is no separation.

The separation came as part of your ego, and said, "Oh you must be careful of what you trust and who you trust and how you trust, oh, my goodness." Where's the love? Trust and Love are the same. So breathe deeply into who you really are. Trust that you already have all you need to know, that it is all inside of you now. Just breathe into the trust and love that you are.

Release your fear. Release your fear and agony. Release the terror that is inside of you like a dagger. Seek your trust in the love and the joy that is abundant and around you. We love you, we support you, know that all you need to do is ask, and we shall talk to you.

Know that Joy is your measure. Joy is the signal from the soul that you are doing exactly what you need to be doing. Joy is a practice; it is a choice. Each thought or feeling that impedes your Peace is to be cast away.

***

There is plenty of evidence in our world to support fear. But the experience of joy or fear results merely from where we place our attention. That is, it is a matter of perspective. If we place our life energy into our ego, our personality-self, then we will always find something to react to in fear. We might experience a temporary pleasure, but the ego's desires never produce lasting peace. Placing your attention on your God-self, your soul, opens the doors to deep Peace and Joy. These are the natural feelings that accompany our authenticity.

We are Spiritual beings having this human experience, individually and collectively. The mass consciousness does influence our experience. Like a captivating Hollywood movie, our attention is often captured and manipulated and we have lost track of what is real. Relax into allowing yourself the gift of engaging in Self-Ascension practices that open your awareness to your Authenticity. Any practice that stills the mind and opens the heart will help you. Find a practice that works for you and make it part of your daily Self-Ascension experience. Several practices are found in this text and in the appendix. There are many others.

Returning Home means returning to your essential Authenticity. Take steps to reduce or eliminate external influence to cultivate a deeper relationship within your self. Waste no time with distractions! Limit television and computer time, turn off offensive music. Stop viewing movies that promote violence, fear and sensationalism. Stop reading the newspaper daily. Stop spending time with fear-filled people. In short, take a vacation from what is considered to be normal! Create the space in your life for your Authenticity to shine through.

The time spent in dialogue with Kiel has provided us with the nudge, the invitation, to step effortlessly and Joyfully into the Authentic immortal self. This is the process of conscious Self-

Ascension. For Ascension is but a remembering of the truth of your being and trusting the knowing. *Only love exists. Let all that is unlike love fall away.*

Welcome home! The lights are on, and the celebration surrounds you. Love is everywhere.

***

[Kiel states] The Elohim speak: "Know that you are loved. Know that you are born of love and are love, have been and always will be love. Learn to simply trust, and we also understand that you may not" [learn to trust].

Self-Ascension is the ability to embody unconditional love with yourself so that you can hold the light for others when they are confused and do not know what is happening. This is not a mission of recognition, platitude or gratitude to the ego; this is one of true service to the six billion who are all coming home. All six billion, for there is no difference.

We are all travelers on this what you call a planet, we have put this [the planet] here as part of the evolution of the soul. You have been here many, many times. You are here now by choice. You chose to be here specifically for this time. Which is why your activation has already begun. It is why you chose your parents and your situations. Move into your flow.

It is important to understand your experience of those that make you uncomfortable or those that do not agree with what you have. The irony is, if they don't agree, then you must have a judgment that they should agree. Not

SRK: An opportunity to negotiate/communicate to all get our needs met.

The opportunity to negotiate is an important one as long as it is framed or established that the only reason for meeting is to agree how we can harmoniously exist on the planet without the interference of each other. For [you] try to interfere. That is the [current] basis of the negotiation. It is not a question of who wins; it is a question of the acknowledgment of everyone's right to exist!

Everyone has the right to their own path, and everyone has the right to their own destiny, the opportunity to take care of that which they need in a manner that is consistent with the path of the individual, yet you are all being interfered with constantly.

It is important to understand that everyone has the right to exist. And no one has the right to decide how. And so you say to me, "What of a society?" I understand, for as society had been designed originally, if you were in a constant allegiance to God and the love of the universe, there would not have been a need for your rules. Because it is just known. I know this may sound simple now.

Because of the imbalance of the dark, and the establishment of the time, the rules had been needed. Originally the rules were truly served by those who truly served. It was designed as a true means of protection and nurturance, for that is the only real vocation, is it not?

SRK: Like guidelines for a child.

What happened was as the mutation continued and as they, [the travelers], became more dependent, the misconception of the service became powerful.

For you see, the mind, not the man, the mind got smart. The mind decided that like a computer that turns on it's inventor, it would be able to control the planet because man had given the power to the mind.

It is simply a computer that has gone wild and it was due to our inability to love ourselves that we thought it would be simpler to give our control to the mind.

...and so now look how far we have come.

First we give our control to this vessel, and to come back and experience here [on this planet], which was meant to be a pure experiment of expression and evolution in the physical form. Then, because it was not always as simple as we wanted it to be, we found we could make it easier to give our power to our computer, our mind, and so we give our power to our mind. Now we are so smart that we have removed ourselves even more from the connection by giving our power over to the artificial mind that we have now created.

What a wonderful way to allow the disconnection from the divine! You are now two times removed! Instead of the man being served by the mind, the computer, and whatever else, it is just the reverse, it is what is leading to the environment of decisions based on ratios and not love. Decisions are being made based upon who has the greatest power force, who has the most money, and who has the best influence to convince others to think their way.

For these are all great sins, the abuse of the power, the abuse of the money, and the abuse of interference with another's karma, which there is no greater sin. It is because of the desire to want to "be" that man's greed and ego can be purchased. And so it has been. And so you must release this. And it brings us back to the, "Oh my god, I am losing my mind... Oh my god, what do I do?"

You let it, [the ego], go!

SRK: Yes, we have our free will.

Absolutely. Yet please understand that you live in a society that has made that last piece by far the most challenging one. For it is in the face of everything that you must take the allegiance to the divine, to your authentic self.

There is only one allegiance, to simply be who you are, to be willing to say, "I am releasing all, including that which I love the most," for even that is a perception.

When you are able to stand in the face of that release, in that moment, is when the love that will come to you is greater than any love you could have ever experienced, and then you are able to truly love the beloved before you and you are truly able to love those around you and recognize the absolute perfection of the divine evolution.

SRK: Then our purpose in working with you and in bringing the book and the teachings is to help prepare the mind?

To help prepare the soul! In the preparation of the soul the mind must be released, and so the first is to prepare yourself so that you can understand what it is and what it feels like and what you go through in the release of the mind, [the ego], for if we were preparing the mind we would still be giving the power to the computer, [the mind], would we not?

SRK: This is so.

In preparing the soul you are being given steps, relax and allow yourself to let the information flow and trust. In so doing, you will be blessed with everything you would ever need or ever want.

SRK: Yes.

You are so loved, so supported, and so protected, you have been given everything you have asked for and yet the mind is wanting to know when the other shoe will fall, is this right?

SRK: Yes.

The piece that is important to understand is what you felt like when everything you asked for was in front of you and it was not longer a game to play but a life to live. That is the difference.

Everything up to this point in your life has been a game. This is not to discount or discredit it at all. It simply means that as it has been, it has been part of the evolutionary process. And so like a game, you simply advance to the next round.

Yet, when you finally start living the integration of the advancing of the rounds it is terrifying.

You don't know what to do. You are in the condition of the game. You are in the condition of the way it should look. You are in the condition of the way your relationship should look, your work should look, your home should look; the way your life should look. It is important for you to know that it is exactly what it needs to look like and you are prepared to be the teacher of others. Who better to teach than the one who is walking through it himself?

You see you do not need to be the expert that your mind deludes you to believe. It is your smoke screen to stop you from the connection. This is where your mind holds you captive, you continually input even more. Your computer [mind] is very strong and is that not perfect? For you will have others with computers that are also strong and those whose computers are not so strong. Because of your strength, you will not take advantage and you will not abuse, and you will serve. How could you do all this without being exactly who you are now?

Section Four

Be in Union

Children's eyes, birds' songs,
Laughter, flowers and floating clouds
Each teases the passion
That resides inside.

Is life but endless foreplay,
God's brilliant plan to seduce
All who inhale deeply
Into Celestial Union?

Let us become
One Smile
One Breath
One Heart
One Sigh.

Walk in Beauty!

Sri Ram Kaa

Special Introduction to Section Four

Spiritual Practices for Daily Living to Achieve Self-Ascension

Many of us have separated so far from our God-self that we do not recognize it. Begin connecting to your Authenticity by watching your feelings. If you are not experiencing Peace, Love, or Joy, then change your priorities. Anything less than Peace and Joy is a sign that your ego is overly involved. This is an important step for many who have busy lives. Make space for your Authenticity to come forward.

The point of daily practice is to open your experience to allow the *essential* to enter. This means bringing spiritual truth more fully into your waking consciousness. Self-Ascension practice is returning to "home" every time you catch yourself having a negative thought. Through prayer, meditation, song, chants, art, yoga, soul nourishment, mindfulness, and similar practices, we provide our Authentic selves an opening and thereby purify our lives (our egos). Through spiritual practice, we invite an ever-greater richness of the love of the Divine to enter and partake in our life experience.

The next time you feel self-doubt, fear or pain, decide right then to thank those feelings for catching your attention. Stop what you are doing, put your hand over your heart and really feel the pain of the situation for a moment. Then ask yourself, *is this true about me?* Your inner child (your ego) may respond, *Yeah, it's true, I'm flawed,* or, *I don't belong.* Then call forth your soul, your own capacity for unconditional love. Send some love to that hurting part of you and say, *I hear you and I love you,* but I am bigger than that point of view. I am a Divine Being, filled with Love and creativity. I am the child of the Most High. I claim my Truth now.

Inhale Love, exhale Love, breathe deeply and keep doing this until you relax into the truth of your Being. You are love. You are the canvas upon which the drama of pain and fear is being played out. You are not the pain or fear, you are indeed bigger than that. Practice moving your consciousness into the fullness of who you truly are.

Once you have relaxed into the truth of love, you can then change your orientation. Begin by choosing Joy. State it out loud. *I choose Joy now.* Let a smile come to your lips. If you do not feel the shift ask yourself: *What point of view is required to create joy right now?* Then you might ask, *What is keeping me from changing my point of view right now?*

Try it. You can change your point of view. Joy is a choice. It just requires a little practice. From the energy of Joy, you will uncover fresh solutions to all your challenges.

Consciousness is like water. It will take on the color of your thoughts and feelings. This is another reason why it is so important to limit your exposure to sensationalism, such as the popular media. Spiritual practice is a method of clarifying the waters. While some religions are associated with certain particular practices, know that the spiritual practices are not owned by anyone. When my mother first heard that I meditated, she assumed that I was now a Buddhist! You don't have to change your religion to import a spiritual practice into your daily life!

As you move further into living your Authenticity, we simply remind you that there are no external rules. Release anything that feels like struggle for you in the daily celebration of your God connection. Struggle is a sign that you are trying to conform or adapt in a way that is not Authentically you.

Looking deeply into the eyes of your Beloved is a good way to enjoy an ever-expanding recognition of their divinity. Gazing deeply dissolves barriers, opens hearts and allows Love to heal. Take some time each day to sit knee-to-knee with your Beloved. Hold their hands and gaze into their eyes. Simply *be* together. As you gaze into their eyes know that this beautiful Being is the Beloved. Hide nothing, for only love exists in Sacred Union. This exercise can lead to quiet sharing and the practice of being Transparent[9] and Present each to each.

During this time of rapid acceleration in our lives, many find that confusion, frustration and discomfort show up regularly. You do not have to tolerate this. Rather than focus on your lack of clarity, simply sit comfortably, relax, and listen to your heart. Breathe slowly for a few moments while holding your attention on your heart center. If you have been hiding your emotions they may show up! Let your own sacred heart show you the love that you are. After you have taken a moment to connect with your heart then allow this question to enter into your consciousness:

---

[9]See Chapter on Transparent Communication

If it doesn't look like joy, why am I doing it?

Simply pausing to ask the question may be enough to shift your experience. If you still feel heavy and serious after asking the question, then you may need to journal a bit about all your good reasons for feeling miserable!

- ❤ Am I doing it because I feel obligated?
- ❤ Am I doing it solely for approval?
- ❤ Am I doing it because I know it is *good* for me?
- ❤ Am I doing it because someone told me that it was the right thing to do?
- ❤ Do I believe that I have no other choice?

Spend as much time as you need every day reviewing your answers, going to ever further depths into your beliefs and actions. You are getting to know yourself. You are uncovering *your* truth. At the end of each session, acknowledge yourself for the effort. Say out loud:

Thank you for loving me. Thank you for sharing with me. I chose to love who I am in this moment without judgment.

This practice is also helpful to adopt when you feel someone has hurt you or violated your trust. Rather than remaining in fear, hate, or anger, do the Star practice (see Appendix) for a few minutes until you feel calm. Ask yourself what point of view you need to adopt in order to feel Joy right now? After answering that question, allow yourself to experiment and try out that point of view.

Every feeling is a gift. Every unpleasant experience is an opportunity to gain in clarity and self-compassion. There is a difference between effort and struggle. You do need to make the effort to evolve, to learn and discern. It does take effort to step out of life-long habits. Struggle, on the other hand, is experienced when you have already given up and there is no Joy in the efforting. Struggle is a signal that your Authenticity wants you elsewhere!

The end of day practice is simple: just appreciate yourself! Review the events of the day and celebrate and appreciate whatever you accomplished, big or small. Whatever you accomplished is truly what your soul called you to accomplish. Have no judgment, simply appreciate the experience of the day. Avoid dwelling on what you did not accomplish, this leads you to a state of separation. Kiel reminded us that by remaining focused on our accomplishments and feeling Joy and appreciation, we are healing the structures of separation. Allowing our authenticity to shine ever more fully in day-to-day life experiences.

Integration of this simple yet highly effective bedtime practice will continue the escalation of your vibratory level and Self-Ascension. Remember, only Love exists!

While the focus of these exercises has been predominately spiritual in nature, it is important to remember that physical movement of the body is just as important. Kiel reminds us often to nourish ourselves! Nourishment is not just about food; it is also about vibratory health for body and soul. A daily routine of soul-centered movement is optimal. As with all other practices, it should have a love energy and God focus. We have found that walking (preferably outdoors) and yoga are two optimal venues to accomplish this. When walking, breathe deeply and enjoy a rhythm. If you practice yoga, remember that each posture is a prayer, not a goal. Be in the wholeness of the practice. The intent is communion.

Consider movement time as an opportunity to reconnect and to provide you with the experience of Peace, Love, and Joy. Creating an environment of fast-paced, over-exerted physical activity will not accomplish this. The goal of the exercise is to stimulate health and to further integrate your Authentic self with your vessel, not to polish your self-image. You honor God as you honor yourself.

In summary, soul nourishment is really very simple...so simple that it is challenging for the western mind! Eat natural foods, drink pure water, step out into fresh air for movement and breathing, allow the sun to bathe your skin, cultivate the energy of gratitude and love throughout the day and remember God through devotion, prayer and meditation.

Kira Raa and I have created a Temple in our home. It is a sacred space where we meditate, sing and offer healing energy to others. We pray there twice daily. Our temple offers recognition of the universality of God's creation. We respect all religions and honor them in our sacred space. We have found God in every religion into which we have looked. God is not hiding!

We recommend that you create sacred space in your home by bringing into it special objects that remind you of God; objects that help you create the energy of reverence. Devotion and Joy help you celebrate your divinity. Your temple can be a space on a bookshelf, a table in the corner of a room, or a whole room. All that matters is the sincerity of practice you bring to it.

As shown in the Self-Ascension Model, the path of Self-Ascension moves you through three states of consciousness. It is a never-ending ever-refining cycle. These are reiterated below.

The Path of Self-Ascension is paved with Peace, Love and Joy.

Peace *Knows* God

Love *Connects* with God

Joy *Embraces* God

9

Sex, Healing, and Divine Union

In the world of duality everything is a relationship. In the world of oneness, everything is love. Self-Ascension involves breathing the oneness into form and allowing all that is unlike love to melt away.

❧

Just relax, do not try to strive. Just listen...

In the beginning, when the vessels were created, they were created in imperfection of the union with the Soul that the experience of evolution could be as full and complete as possible. And so, it was important to have the misconceptions. It was important to not be able to fully interpret so it would create the environment for the growth and the searching and the understanding through the evolutionary process. You are coming home. For that is what is happening.

SRK: The imagery that's in my awareness right now is of the emerging of Authenticity. That the fullness of the Authenticity is one of the soul's life. The soul's recognition permeating the illusion, permeating the separation, and unifying with matter. I see this as a glowing, a fullness, a ripening, so to speak. Instead there has been a duration where we have gone sideways into further and further darkness, further and further separation. That mis-direction of our energies has been one of further convolutions of the external, convolutions of separation.

Yes. This has strengthened the ego. And in doing so has strangled this sphere, strangled the gift to the point that we now require a more energetic transformation as opposed to the more peaceful process of evolution that was started. And so it is still the same process of awakening, it's just more shocking, in a sense, to the status quo....to release the ego.

SRK: It's simple; just release the ego.

Correct. Are not your miracles unfolding in front of you? Was not it a miracle that the Kira Raa could move through an incredibly difficult, challenging, traumatic experience with your assistance and our assistance in very little time? Was that not a miracle? Was that not your burning bush?

SRK: Yes, it cleared in so little time.

> Note: Kiel is referring to the clearing of a painful childhood trauma. Many people have experienced traumatic events that create lasting imprints in their psyches. By offering this imprint into the crucible of the divine relationship, it was healed. The post-traumatic stress was dissolved through transparency and the application of divine love. We have omitted details of the dialogue and the techniques involved because we feel it is inappropriate for the scope of this book.

There are many, many, many people who have been through this [trauma]. This is why the Kira Raa had to go through all of this, just as you have gone through a lot of your own pain. If you had not experienced this yourselves, you would not be capable of being the teachers of the teachers.

SRK: I have another question. When we were in the desert you mentioned that you would talk about sex.

We would prefer to discuss this sex as the physical union. It is the physical union of the vessels. And it is the expression of joy of the vessels and one that further enhances the energetic pattern between the Beloved couples. It is a necessary component. This is another thing that brings you so much closer to your Authenticity. This is why it has been controlled by those in some religions as being "bad" and not "good." Yes, there is much abuse of this, which is really a part of people just looking to find the connection to their authenticity. It is simply the twisting of this. They are so eager to find their authenticity they do not even know why they are abusing it. It is because they hunger and crave to reconnect.

SRK: Someone has once written that sex is the only form of meditation that many know.

This is very true because it is a reaching out. It is a prayer.

SRK: It is the dissolving of the ego...for an instant, perhaps.

Absolutely. And it is looking for the reconnection to the authentic self. For as the Beloved couples come together it is a way to truly remain connected. Couples that release this [sex], lose their connection with each other. Some believe they are actually furthering their union with God, yet they are separating and isolating from each other. Is that truly union? If the physical vessel is not supported with continuous energetic and vibrational love on the physical level, why have the vessel? It is an expression of authenticity. It is a means by where your authentic selves can meet. The vibrations can be raised through the physical vessels and the vibrations can be joined. It is especially blissful among your soul group, for you are desiring to be back in this union. It is the last means of big control.

SRK: Control?

Control! There are many religions that say in order to be holy you must not have sex. What irony! For that has caused much abuse. For even those holy people are trying to connect to their authenticity and of course they are searching for it. This has been abused much and is just now coming to the surface.

SRK: Yes, suppression of a natural impulse can become perverse.

Correct.

SRK: But also, I see the practice of controlling the sexual impulse as useful at some stages of learning. For example, exercising the will or getting in touch with the spiritual body at the expense of the integration of all the bodies.

Discernment needs to be used. Because in the physical union of the vessels whether you are with the Beloved or not, there is an exchange of your energy. And there is a release and it does touch in some manner. Therefore, discernment is important. It is important to understand that the physical union is truly designed for the enhancement of the authentic soul. Anything other than this is not of the highest service. It is simply being done for the pleasure of the physical body similar to when you crave a chocolate! And so it is important to understand that in the union of the Beloved it is perfectly natural and acceptable to have this craving with each other and to satisfy it. There is nothing wrong with this! There is nothing that is not sacred. For is it not wonderful to be in the union with the Beloved?

SRK: Is there a depletion of energy when one is having sexual union with an inappropriate—that might be too harsh a word- with the "wrong" energetic partner?

With one other than the Beloved partner?

Depletion is not the word for that implies a loss. What there is, is an energy exchange that will keep your vibrational level lower and therefore simply create an opportunity for you to move through. It is very similar to eating foods that keep you in the wrong space. It is very much "food" [sexual union].

Expand the definition. It is part of the sustenance of the vessel. It is very true that when this piece of the vessel is not used many suffer physical manifestations that have yet to be further discovered by what you call your medical community. They, [the medical community], have their own concerns about integrating the lack of union to those physical ailments that plague your society. The prostate problems in many is very largely due to lack of union. It is due to lack of union with the Beloved and the combination of many years of guilt and suffering for inward desires which are turned into other manifestations instead of the authentic expression with the Beloved. This is why the prostate problem grows so heavily in this country. There is also for women breast cancer. Breast cancer manifests for many reasons. Yet there are energies that must be sustained throughout the feminine body that can only be achieved through the union with the Beloved. If the studies would look at the sexual union habits among the men with the prostate and the women with the breast cancer, (this is especially true in the age group 45 and above), you will find direct correlation.

SRK: Let me see if I understand this. In the age group 45 and above you are suggesting there is a lack of the sacred exchange?

When the lack exists is when the force of being able to truly find authenticity reduces and therefore the energies find a mutation in the body. For men it is in the prostate and for women it is in the breast. If you are observant, you will notice couples that are in their authenticity and regularly in union and the couples that are not.

SRK: Yes, an essential vitality is missing.

Absolutely. It radiates. It also affects the manner in which the mind and the ego operate. For when you lack the physical union with the Beloved, the ego becomes stronger...it becomes more "I" centered. It is also searching and frustrated and therefore seeks to control. It will ardently try to create scenarios in the mind that support why this is not happening, thereby strengthening the ego even more, creating even further separation.

SRK: Yes, that is marvelous. The ego searches for the antidote to its existence!

Absolutely correct. The ego will do anything. The ego is the greatest, slyest, pirate on the planet. It will use any means possible and steal anything possible to justify its existence and become even greater and stronger. And it has no concern for your authentic self.

SRK: Yet the impulse of it is divinely inspired to lead us to our sacred selves.

Absolutely. But even that is convoluted for the ego does not even recognize what it is doing. And that is in its design. In a society...I do not want to limit this to the society in which you are sitting in now...On this sphere, the physical union has been one of the most powerful methods of control. There have been many ego-written texts and documents about what is acceptable and what is not acceptable. Understand this: that which provides joy between the Beloved couples is acceptable. There is none that can govern sexual joy, except the couple themselves.

SRK: So you are now speaking to sexual practices. I understand what you are saying, but the place my mind goes next is the promiscuity, the experimentation, the having of many partners.

I am not referring to that.

SRK: I know that is not what you were addressing a moment ago, but is that not a response, a reaction to the over-control?

Absolutely. Once you are in the sacred relationship, if you are truly bound by the authenticity, all of that is unnecessary. It all folds into the same explanation we talked about a moment ago. It was all just looking for their authenticity that it brought them to. And if the end result is to be with their Beloved, was it so terrible?

SRK: No, it is the development of discernment.

Thank you.

SRK: And for those that fail to develop discernment it becomes an addiction.

Correct. Then, like any other addiction it is a question of how it is moved through. So understand this: there can not be any judgment around the practices of the sexual unless they cause harm. For it is never to cause harm. And even then we can not judge, we can simply allow a healing process.

SRK: Does compulsive activity of the ego in its searching result in addictive behavior? In psychology I was taught that many of those who have received inappropriate sexual contact when they were young compulsively search out sexual partners in later life. It's as if that energy of sexuality is seeking resolution of the trauma through sexual expression.

That is an ego-centered definition. When the trauma exists, it is different for all and therefore it cannot be categorized automatically. Some will do as you just described. Some will not. However, there is nothing to be concerned about within the union of the Beloved. There are those that have a higher need to express...this is just who they are.

SRK: So in the presence of the Beloved there will be a natural progression, and I think rapid evolution toward authenticity.

And balance.

SRK: That magnetism, that completion and balance of being with the appropriate sacred vessel is healing.

Correct.

SRK: So the real essence, then the early teaching, is how to recognize and find the Beloved.

That is correct. That is why it is important to be teaching the younger. A day ago you were questioning about teaching the younger generation.

SRK: And that is sacred.

Yes, it is. We appreciate your acknowledgment.

SRK: So the younger generation, are they not of a different soul group[10]? Are most of them coming on the planet now or that have come on the planet in the past 20 years of a soul group that does not require a partner to know God? Or are there many of my soul group?

There are many.

SRK: Many in both?

Yes, and the ones that are coming in now are already Masters. That is why there is such a strong shift between the way children are raised and perceived and what they understand and know. Their function is to help raise the vibratory level for not only the planet, but for their parents. They are here for rapid escalation purposes. That is why many of all ages are bringing in children. There are those that are even more linear older than you, Sri Ram Kaa that are bringing in children.

SRK: It is all serving the evolution of the planet?

---

[10]Kiel has explained that there are several distinct soul groups on the planet and has asked that they be fully discussed in Book Two.

It is all about the raising of the level. Preparing everyone. All six billion are coming home. How they come home will be different.

SRK: So then what I am hearing this as, is a continuation of the evolutionary opportunity such as this sphere provided?

Correct. It is just in a whole new way.

SRK: Fair enough. Then my role is to serve as a light of awakening for those who are in the place to accept that?

Correct! Simple and Correct. As is the role of the Kira Raa. And as is the role of Self-Ascension.

SRK: And so the fact that I love those and feel that I wish to make myself available to even those who do not want me…

That is ego or that is you?

SRK: (laughs) There is a paradox that I felt of wanting **all** to experience the joy of union and the acceptance that not all will have this experience and yet really wanting to try and…(SRK begins laughing loudly)—it *is* ego!

That is funny. It is interesting to watch this process in you. It is important that you continue cellular cleansing. Your healing is necessary and in process. You have spent too much time with physical constraints. It has taken away from your ability to go deeper. Continue with meditation. You are much loved. Remember to be grateful. You have much. Release your fears; move into the trust. Follow the model. Live it. All will be provided.

Live in Joy. Embrace in Joy. Simply be grateful to breathe and see the sun and know the colors and expressions. Delight when your Beloved wants to provide you Joy. Delight in providing Joy for your Beloved. Delight in the small things. Delight in all. That is what this evolution is about.

Know this: We love you. Know that we love you. Know that we support you. Know that all is truly well. Know that your authenticity is so vibrantly beautiful that there is only love and that you will be abundantly cared for.

Kiel's teachings were accelerating our evolution. The journey Kira and I embraced with Kiel has brought us many remarkable experiences. During the first 45 days, we experienced a deepening of our Authenticity in stages and with each gain came a response from the ego. Fears arose. I would feel so peaceful and blessed following a morning discourse with Kiel and by the afternoon I experienced frustration, resistance and pain. I was often judgmental of Kira. This was painful for us both, **for nothing erodes Joy faster than judgment.** Yes, we both still had our egos! We both had ego habits.

Yet, the love was there. The soul love ran deep and each time I retreated into my process, my unspoken judgments, we both experienced emotional pain. There is no hiding from the Beloved. You are either in Joy experiencing love or you are in pain. Sometimes pain is experienced as the numbness of denial.

So each occurrence of pain flushed out hidden judgments or unexpressed fears. Each occurrence of pain, if brought into open discussion, could be loved into wholeness very quickly. This is the power of Transparency. The loving energy of the Sacred Union is amazingly healing. Years of habits began to dissolve. Patterns of fear learned in childhood quickly softened.

At first the progress toward living in Joy seemed slow. In the first couple of weeks there were times when I thought about ending the relationship, times when I doubted myself, my Beloved, and Kiel. It seemed ridiculous to see the same doubts and fears keep arising. The Sacred Union had upped the ante. I thought I was evolved, but when paired with my perfect mirror, a new layer of shadow was revealed! We discovered the substance that had been lurking behind the curtain of consciousness. In the Sacred Union, both your Authenticity and your ego become more visible. At first this felt like a roller coaster. We traveled the terrain of inner peace, spiritual visions and Joy to feelings of fear, anxiety, doubt and dread.

Dread is the most vicious weapon of the ego. First it summons self-doubt by bringing in thoughts of impending doom, which generates feelings of fear and a touch of confusion. The cycle spins, ever- tightening its grip on your stomach. Then the ego offers a solution to the very problem it manufactured. *Just follow this simple plan,* it says. *Revert back to the known territory, the way it was.* The ego would have you tuck your tail between your legs and run!

Every spiritual traveler has experienced this shenanigan. And eventually, we all learn that there is no turning back. The ego, however, has no regard for the prior lessons of the soul. The ego will throw many distracting thoughts up on the screen of consciousness with the hope that the emotions generated will stop the actualization of the soul. The key is to smile. The key is to be able to love the mechanism that generates negative thoughts, resistance, confusion and fear, for what can be loved can be healed.

There is nothing that love cannot heal, nothing. Every creation in this universe has the energy of love as its essential matrix. That which does not look like love, that which does not feel like love *is illusion.*

By the end of the year, only seven weeks after joining my life with Kira, I was able to start laughing at my ego-shenanigans. The uprisings of resistance were few, the depth of everyday joy increased and the flow of remarkable coincidences increased. Yes, amazing things occurred in a very short time. My sleep apnea had disappeared, Kira's antidepressants were discontinued, excess weight was dissolving, clarity and enthusiasm were heightened, and abundance was enhanced.

We enjoyed these tangible miracles in the first ninety days of Authentic living. There was no dieting, no exercise, nothing, but moving into the energy of Authentic Union. Yes, these were miracles.

From the viewpoint of your Authenticity, the real miracle is our ability to believe in something less than perfect health and Joy! The *miracle* is that as powerful children of the Most High we actually fear others and attempt to destroy them. Yet, the Creator has allowed our distortions to drive our experiences out of sheer respect for our free will, out of unconditional love for us and our chosen method of evolution. The problem is we have forgotten that pain is a choice.

When we view something with fear or anger, when we judge something as unacceptable, we have suspended the energy of healing. It does not matter whether we are viewing an aspect of ourselves or another person. The moment we judge, the moment we resist or retreat, that is the moment healing energy is cut off.

Old age is a bad joke. The body may age, but health, humor and joy do not depend upon any outside condition. They depend only upon inner alignment. Once you truly embrace your spiritual truth, then the vessel and the human experience shifts in a good way. The outer world becomes supportive and entertaining. Joy becomes the predominate emotion. Life becomes an ever-expansive opportunity to know love through service.

This joy is not just for the few. Bliss and serenity are not just for the spiritually accomplished. They are your birthright. Like the prodigal son, each of us will be given the kingdom when we return home. Home is not a geographical location; it is a state of consciousness.

We are all travelers. To travel means to visit this beautiful sphere called Earth and cycle through seemingly endless reincarnations of forgetfulness. For a spiritual Being to identify with dense matter and set aside its glory is an amazing act of courage. You are that Being. You are *that* courageous.

Returning home requires trust, courage and devotion. These are the tools that dissolve the grip of the ego. No special certificate of training is needed. No passport is required, no vaccinations, no "paying your dues." You have already proven your worth, simply by showing up.

My fears and doubts lessened with time. Each time fear or resistance to the flow arose, I was given an opportunity to love myself, to resolve a limiting belief, and to surrender. If we run from fear, it is endless; if we embrace fear, we will dissolve it.

The ego is not our enemy, it is our challenge, for the very device that provides the structure and friction necessary for our evolution has grown out of proportion. The ego is to serve us, not hinder our authentic expression. Once fear is dissolved, the negative qualities of the ego fade away. What remains is a tool for discernment and experience, a vehicle for enhancing joy while in the physical.

Union does not require a mate. Union does not require another person. The essence of Sacred Union is the conscious connection to God. The Beloved is communication with God either directly or with a partner. Some may find that their partner is not presently in a body, yet they can enjoy communion via meditation.

It is the time of activation of the Sacred Unions. Being called back together to bring balance to the energy of the planet. In the Union, there is no fear. Release of Time is essential to enjoy

Union. The Union is completion. It means that your travels are over. If you are called to Union it means that you are preparing to help others ascend, for Union is the completion of the evolutionary design of the earth school. Many souls do not require a partner to commune with The Elohim. Confusion about the need for a partner is the source of pain for many. Align your chakras[11] together, then be in Union, breathe as one breath.

What most people refer to as a Soul Mate is actually a Karmic Mate. This relationship is characterized by a magnetic attraction and perhaps a sense of resolution. The Sacred Union, on the other hand, is characterized by a sense of completion. It has never happened before so the feelings and perceptions may be unlike anything you have ever experienced.

Some of you have been with your appropriate partner for years. You may find that your relationship needs work because you have failed to fully embrace the Sacred Union. That is, your Sacred Union may not have been activated at the time you were married. The activation process on this planet only began a few years ago. So take heart! You have the opportunity to delve deeper into intimacy with your partner, if you so choose.

Coupleship can be a wonderful experience if the parties know how to surrender to love. If the relationship feels empty, flat or incongruent with your inner yearnings, then it is time to take an honest look at the relationship. Are there unexpressed emotions that have become rotting resentments? Repressed feelings will dull any relationship. Are you uncertain about your true feelings? Sometimes we do not want to face our inner feelings because we are afraid that to do so will result in greater pain or embarrassment. Many of us hide our true feelings from ourselves and others because we learned in childhood that only positive emotions would be well received by others. The result is that we disown a portion of ourselves.

Whatever the reason, your life is *your* life. You get to experience the result of your choices, whether those choices are conscious or not! So, the faster you become conscious of your truth, the faster you will experience freedom, authentic power and Joy.

---

[11]Chakras are subtle energy centers that emanate from the spine.

Love is for everyone. Love is inescapable. It is everywhere. Yet, in spite of this truth, many are afraid that they will never find love again if they leave their relationship. Love is everywhere. Loving people are everywhere. If you love yourself, then you will attract loving people into your life. If you are hiding some ancient feelings of shame or are in the habit of being self-deprecating, then your friends will probably mirror the same fears that cripple you.

You deserve every ounce of Joy you can carry. Joy knows not doubt, shame, illness, or depression. Joy is not a goal that you hope to attain after you have put the kids through college. Joy is not the destination. Joy is the path. If repressed emotions are blocking your Joy, then pursue whatever feels right for you to uncover those feelings.

If you love your Self, you are loving the child of the Creator. That is a sacred act! To love yourself is to love God. To celebrate yourself is to celebrate God! It is not prideful or selfish to seek what you want. What is important is that you also honor that everyone has the same right to authentic self-expression. Everyone has the right to get their needs met.

<hr/>

There is a mistake among the belief that union is only man/woman. As man/woman you will be in balance and show balance [of masculine and feminine energy]. But you are symbolic balance. For balance is attained through love. There are many expressions of love and we shall talk about what love truly is. For on this world or planet there has been a great misunderstanding of love. It is imperative that the model of male-female be the energy that heals the planet; which is why you and the Kira have been instructed to Union.

If a man loves another man, if a woman loves another woman, if any one person loves merely God, it is the balance and the love, as we will discuss it, that matters. It is the union that is the divine. You have been brought into perfect union as an example. Union is blessed, all union. The concept of shame, the concept of guilt, and the concept of wrong, serve only for your evolution. Once you have attained the Union, you would not need to know what wrong is by the definition of another, because you are vibrating at the level of Union, of love. At this vibrational level, you are only able to serve in joy and in great splendor to withstand all circumstances. For all are evolving.

It is very important for us to understand that the Divine is also expressed through sexual union. We are each a unique embodiment of the Divine. While there are universal spiritual principles that apply to us all, the path we take to awaken is unique. Sacred relationship does not require a male and a female. Sacred relationship refers to the intention of the parties, not their gender. Same sex partnerships also embody the principles of Sacred relationship.

All judgment around "good" and "evil" is a human creation. All systems of evaluation are of the ego. It is important to recognize that those systems may be useful in some ways for organizing human society into predictable patterns of behavior. This generates a feeling of safety for some. However, those patterns are not set down from on High. God does not judge. God only expects that we will return home.

Just as we see the Divine wrapped in the clothing of wondrous ethnic diversity, we also see the Divine in each gender. Sexual expression is the interaction of the masculine and the feminine energies and does not require the clothing of a particular gender in order to reach fullness.

The criteria for self-discernment is simply this: do the energy signatures of the souls match? This has nothing to do with age, race, or gender. In a true match, there will be an essential compatibility, as evidenced by a sense of peace or completeness when the partners are together.

Our sexual signature is not the sex act. It is an energy. The sex act is a beautiful exchange and blending of energy with that of our partner. It is sacred, holy, and healthy for the individuals who participate in Sacred Union. It nourishes the body as well as the soul.

The soul learns through contrast. Thus each of us here has been both the victim and the offender. We could not become saints if we did not know how to sin. Many of us learn to respect the sex act by first being disrespectful of the sanctity of that energy exchange.

Sex between sacred partners enriches each. If one of the partners chooses to have sexual relations with someone else, they have diluted themselves. They have mingled their energies with someone who is less compatible. This mingling may be informative or enjoyable to the ego, but it does not accelerate Self-Ascension. It can, however, serve the evolution of the soul by assisting in the development of discernment. For how can a soul choose a path without understanding the consequences of that choice?

For some soul types, partnership does not enhance their communication with the Elohim. Thus, sexual exchange is simply a celebration. As long as the sexual partner is of a similar vibratory level, there is no energetic detriment to the exchange. For those souls who are created to be in Sacred Union, (approximately 1/3 of the planet's population[12]), there is only one partner who will truly support Self-Ascension. Intermingling with others sidesteps the process.

Conformity is the creation of the ego and an attempt to control. Diversity is a fact of creation. God is infinitely creative. How could sameness result from the infinitely creative? So it is with sexual interactions. Moral prohibitions do not apply across the board. Moral prescriptions can apply universally. True honoring is allowing the other to have their unique path and supporting them to achieve congruence with their inner beliefs and Authenticity.

❦

This is why training in what to expect in the sacred relationship is very important. This training should be started in the teen years, and made available so that all can understand what they are looking to find. As the love is understood as a vital connection to the Divine, the greater the challenge will be to break free of the ego to search with the soul.

There will be those who will be in fear. They are simply in fear because they themselves are so disconnected that they cannot find this love for themselves. They will protect the illusion even more, and so, for them, use the star of your third eye,[13] knowing that you beam them the love. There is only one place where this love exists, in perfect union with the Elohim. This love exists inside of you. It

---

[12]This figure was provided to us by Archangel Zadkiel.

[13]See Appendix: The Star Practice

is inside of all. It must be brought back [to the self], before any transition can occur.

SRK: It brings me peace and joy to know it is all unfolding in perfection.

Yes, between your Peace and Joy, and simply through your own trust and acceptance of your authenticity is the Love. The connection that the authenticity brings is a sense of peace that cannot be explained.

SRK: Yet it was that Peace that helped me recognize my Beloved. When I connected with Kira's energy, I did experience an excitement, but more importantly, what I noticed was a sense of completion, a sense of peace, not a peace in terms of a stillness, but in terms of wholeness. That sense of completion was central in my discernment that this was the One I was looking for.

And so, is not this voice, this sense, love?

SRK: I guess what I am confessing is that I had not understood love in that sense up until experiencing the energy of my Beloved. And so, the energy of the Beloved will be used to fashion a new experience.

Of course.

———

The vessel is not the soul! God sees only the brilliance of the illuminated soul. Find your sacred partner. Love that person. Be in union. Trust. This is the true path of Self-Ascension.

Once one has experienced the nectar of the Divine Union, to whatever degree One has allowed oneself to consciously experience it, then that taste forever alters one's willingness to settle for a lesser peace. Buddha is reported to have said that once an individual has heard of Nirvana, they will seek it, and eventually, find it. So it is with Sacred Union.

It is popular nowadays to talk of finding your soul mate. How do you find your soul mate? What happens when you are no longer compatible with your soul mate? What if you recognize them and they do not recognize you? The drama and discussion of relationship issues is vast and entertaining, for human beings crave security, love and completion.

Each of us carries a Divine longing. Each soul has within it a seed of desire for re-unification with its Creator. This Divine longing is sometimes denied and sometimes misinterpreted. All addiction has at its root a longing, a desire to fill an inner hole with peace. The peace that is sought is truly the Peace of God. Instead, the individual may use substances, activities, or relationships to fill the hole. This will not ever produce lasting peace. Instead of looking at this yearning as a flaw I encourage you to honor your longing as a sacred quest. It is the quest for authenticity. Use the longing to help you step out of unproductive habits and cultivate ever more alignment with your Authenticity.

True Sacred Union has at its center the love of God and the intention to use the Union of the couple to elevate the individual's conscious connection with the Elohim. Thus, the essence of Divine Partnership is that the spiritual evolution of the Beloved is paramount to each individual. It is important that the partners seek to dissolve the veil of separation that is evidenced by the body, the sense of time, illness, death, and other ego-centered dramas.

The quickest way to attain this is through Transparent Communication. It is also the most frightening and requires complete trust.

10

Transparent Communication

What I seek
Cannot be found.

It must simply
Become present.

In me,
Through me,
As me.

Sri Ram Kaa

There is a story within the story. Ascension is the natural process of going home, or residing in your Authenticity as a spark of God. There are many on the planet who now reside in this state of self-realization. We all visit this consciousness during the time between incarnations and then slip into forgetfulness to experience a lifetime in the physical. Kira and I have been blessed with the awareness of our own activation of soul mission.

One morning Kira slipped into a deep coma-like trance and had I not first been prepared by instructions from Kiel, I would have called the paramedics. For the duration of two days I attended to her body while information came to us in both verbal and non-verbal form.

The one of the one of the oneness is guiding. This vessel is in suspended animation. It is your love and attention that keeps it alive. As Oneness grows, as recognition grows, so does the love.

Only love exists here. The female leads with great love into ascension, a true release of the vessel; like death, only an opening, a gift for the male. Release all attachment to gravity and this sphere. Honor nothing that is not love.

If it does not feel or look like love, it should not be done. This applies to everything. Understand what love is. Divine Meditation to the most holy is important [for this understanding].

All relationship is Sacred, for each of us is a splinter of the Divine. Thus, when two Divine splinters come together they create a glow, an enhancement that supports learning about love. This supports learning about the ego and provides the opportunity to play out the lessons and the wounding. All relationship, therefore, is Sacred, extremely vulnerable, and an invaluable lesson for the development of the individual.

However, there was another relationship Kira and I sought: the mystical search. The ecstasy of the dissolving of the separate individual into the heart of God. We wanted to know God through the Union of the Beloved. To see God in the eyes of our partner, and to know the energetic expansion that comes with the sacred sexual union. Kira and I were conscious that we sought a depth of soul connection that traditional standards seldom addressed.

Kira's Journal

He wants me to do what? Hold nothing back, simply say what I am really feeling, when I am feeling it! I feel like the alien who uses telepathy to communicate—only with spoken words. This is a frightening challenge.

I have so wanted to be in a relationship where I could feel safe enough to be truly "naked" with my partner, not in the physical sense, but in the sense of true vulnerability, true connection. I knew this was only possible if I could finally allow myself to truly trust.

For many years I had lamented my many bad marriages and was quite adept at the "poor me" syndrome. Why had I attracted all these husbands who were unable to be present with me? Men who treated my poorly and took me for granted?

And now the answers are again right in front of me. Again, it is about trust. Yes, I must trust my love, yet, more importantly, I must trust myself. If I agree to this transparent communication, I need to trust myself that I will not let old patterns interfere. I need to trust that he is, indeed, being transparent with me.

Then, the most obvious of all was right in front of me. **If not now, when?** Here I have the opportunity to move forward with one that my soul is recognizing in a manner I've never known. I have the chance to move into my soul recognition with a partner!

Yes, even though it is uncomfortable for me now, I am ready for Transparent Communication. I am ready to trust.

⚜

What is Transparency

Transparency is the willingness to disclose your innermost experience(s) to your Beloved. This is not to imply that you must share every sensation or emotion. It does mean, however, that the partners mutually agree to make a commitment not to withhold emotional content or thoughts from each other, because of the fear of a reaction.

Often the reaction we may be fearing the most is our own self-judgment! That is, we become uncomfortable when we fall short of the standards we have set for ourselves. We are afraid to hurt our partner's feelings, or worse yet, anger them.

This withholding creates separation in couples. Separation will breed further separation and the Union will eventually become weak. True Union requires the willingness to face whatever may arise. The more you withhold, the more secrets you have, the more part-time your relationship will be.

True Union is based upon unconditional love. From the energy of love we can accept that our partner is simply having an experience. We can then choose to be present and lovingly witness that experience with them. It is important to cultivate a quality of connection that is detached from the outcome. When we let go of the outcome, we support our partner's process.

Love will heal whatever pain accompanies that experience. One of the true benefits of Union is that our partner may love us at times we are unable to cultivate self-love. It is this loving presence that holds open the space of healing. Transparency thus helps expose and dissolve the shadow-self.

Self-Ascension requires the release of fear. Self-Ascension requires complete trust. If you are unable trust your partner, it is an indicator that you do not trust yourself. Remember, your partner will mirror your own shadow back to you.

The Sacred Union exists for one purpose: the resolution of whatever does not look like love. How fast or how slow you process your unconscious material is up to you. The Union offers the fire of transformation. Once you discover that you are safe, even when sitting in the burning fire, then your personal evolution is swift!

Everything can be healed. Healing requires connection to the Divine energy, which is love. No amount of meditation, psychotherapy or prayer can match the healing power of Sacred Union combined with Transparent Communication. The love that is cultivated in the Union is more powerful than any earthly healing force. The Union creates a portal to God, to Divine love. **Regardless of this power, it is still up to you to cultivate the courage to be vulnerable and stand in the healing fire of the relationship.**

Intimacy Exercise:

Step One:

Sit or stand face to face with your partner. (If you do not have a partner then stare at a photo of a deity or spiritual master). Be close enough to give each other a hug. Close your eyes and bring your dominant hand to your heart. Breathe fully into your belly and relax into your own heart center. Feel your heart and by doing so you will connect with your Authenticity. Do this with eyes closed for two minutes—it may seem like a long time at first.

Step Two:

With your hand on your heart, open your eyes and gaze into the eyes of your partner. Look deeply at this person. Imagine that you are looking into their soul. If you have unexpressed emotions they may surface. Gaze deeply into the eyes of your Beloved. Beam love and acknowledge them through your gaze.

Step Three:

After connecting for a few moments, decide which partner is the receiver and which is the sender. The sender is to be completely out-focused and send unconditional love to the receiver. Look deeply into the eyes of the receiver. Summon the energy of acceptance and love and send it nonverbally to your partner. If your mind wanders then deliberately think loving thoughts such as, *I love you, I respect you, I am grateful for you.*

The receiver's job is just to let that love in. Imagine that you are a flower being nourished by the sunshine. Just breathe in the energy that is coming your way. Tears may come—allow them, however, keep eye contact with your partner. As the energy of love enters you, know that it will flow to wherever it is needed.

After three minutes you can relax for a couple breaths and then switch. The sender becomes the receiver and the exercise repeated. As you practice you may find that you want to do this longer than 3 minutes. That's wonderful!

Advanced technique:

Begin with Step One above.

When you open your eyes, place your right hand on your partner's heart center as they do the same to you. If you each use your right hand then your arms will not cross. By touching your partners' heart you have increased the energetic connection. Leave your hand on the heart of the other for the entire exercise.

Note about emotions.

Some couples have feelings that have not been shared for a long time. This exercise may trigger the release of these emotions. This can be healing provided that the other partner is able to hold a loving presence. Allow yourself to express those feelings non-verbally. If tears come, know that they are a necessary rinsing. If you feel anger, look deeper inside. Anger is always a surface emotion—it is a protector. Look for the hurt or fear that accompanies the anger and allow yourself to feel.

It is important for the partner who is witnessing to quietly beam love to the other. Do not attempt to comfort the other, just send love through your gaze. By being loving and patient you will get to a place of completion with the feelings. Then you can continue with the exercise.

If there is significant unexpressed emotional content, you may need some counseling assistance. There may be unconscious behavior patterns in your relationship that contribute to pain. You will need to explore these feelings and the unmet needs that underlie them.

It is our experience that therapy is often valuable; but should be viewed as a short-term intervention. What is needed, is the cultivation of loving Presence; learning to set aside your own reactivity and reside in an out-focused heart space. This will create the healing energy to benefit your partner. They can then do the same for you. This is the essence of soul based healing: remembering the Love and Peace of your Authentic Being and residing in that knowing.

11

The Yumi Soul

When two people set up housekeeping there is always the chance that tensions will be created. The various little habits individuals bring to the shared home may clash. Fortunately, the toothpaste tube, items left on the counter tops, and general cleanliness habits never triggered much distress for Kira and me.

Perhaps we were focused on bigger issues. That is, we joined our lives in order to experience Expansion. We sought Ascension. This was not because we wanted to leave this beautiful planet, it was because we love God. The love of the Divine is the reason for all creativity. It is the Divine attraction that generates Authentic movement. We came together because our souls sought completion. We live together and work together because it feels good to do so. We came together in order to offer an example.

What is most amazing was that within two weeks of setting up housekeeping we felt like we had always been together. There was an ease in being together unlike anything I had ever experienced with other relationships.

It was in a matter-of-fact conversational mode that I mentioned to Kira one December afternoon: "I was thinking about getting married when we're in California over New Year's."

She replied: "Okay. Are you wanting to include your San Diego family?"

I answered: "Yes, I thought we could get married on the beach."

It was most likely one of the most casual marriage proposals on record. No fanfare, no tension, just alignment.

On Christmas morning as I was conversing with Zadkiel, he spontaneously offered the following:

Every day the strength of this Union grows. Every day the miracles of this Union unfold. You have lately thought of the communion on the physical level called "marriage." The intensity and the energy that will grow after that marriage you have yet to even understand. It is important.

Your selection of the date is correct; it must be honored. For there is much energy supporting you from the Universe. And it will bring in much magical energy that is yet to come. For as much as is here now there is that much more to come. Stand firm in your commitment to move forward in the Light. Stand firm in your commitment to be the messenger that you are. Be the living example of the unified love of the universe. Be the living example of the Joy of the Creator in the creation. Be the living example of the Christmas in the Christmas, of the Christ energy that will move forward every day. For every day is Christ energy; every day is Christmas, every moment is a gift.

Yes, you must be married on earth in bare feet. Bare feet are optimal and very important for you will feel what will come in. The consecration of the two of you must be done outside in the bare feet.

SRK: At sunrise?

Yes. When the energy is the strongest. The marriage is happening in many dimensions at once; many things will line up when this marriage occurs...and the depth of the love that you and the Kira Raa share will only begin to unfold for you. The Love that the two of you share will go deeper every day. The greater you delve into your Oneness, the greater your Joy, the greater your Peace, the greater the Love and the service you provide to those around you

And so it was, at sunrise on January 3, 2003, we consecrated our commitment to each other through the ceremony of marriage. Barefoot on the beach, hand in hand, we knelt before each other, exchanged our vows and merged our souls more fully than before.

I could not have imagined the difference. In the weeks that followed I discovered a deepening in our Love that could only be called a ripening. I felt somehow wider, fuller, and more grounded in our Love. I felt and continue to feel complete, needless, and whole. Marriage with the true Beloved is a spiritual merging that cannot be understood until experienced. When entered into with conscious intent, Sacred Union creates a portal for the cleansing of karma, the dissolution of all forms of pain and separation and the opportunity for Self-Ascension.

Closing thoughts

Many have had the thought: *What is my life purpose?* It is a powerful question. We offer this simple answer to you: the purpose of life is simply "to be." There is nothing *to do* that will bring you to your life purpose. We are here simply *to be* that which we are. As you relax into the truth of this simple statement, your Authenticity comes forward naturally. As you relax into your Being-ness, then the urging of the soul becomes clear. Artistic, educational and career pursuits all unfold effortlessly as you live from your Authenticity.

We are here to evolve. Evolution of the soul is an ever-refining process of Authentic being. It is the path of love. In the most basic sense, earth school is an adventure in separation.

Yes, the antidote to separation is oneness. However, you cannot consciously choose oneness until you have truly experienced separation. Thus, your soul will give you experiences of pain and separation. The intent is that you will learn how to dissolve those polarities and cultivate Peace, Love and Joy.

Spiritual truth is paradoxical. Earth school offers the opportunity to experience the exquisite dance of duality, allowing one to enjoy the interplay of separation and oneness and delight in the paradox. It is our gift to be able to feel the perfection that is expressed through the fabric of duality.

The suffering and fear of humanity provides ample opportunity to practice Unconditional Love. The conditions that surround us are both blissful and challenging. These conditions stimulate the illusion of separation. The Sacred Union provides us with a nurturing vessel to bring the healing energy of Unconditional Love to ourselves and to our partner. The relationship one has with the Beloved is then extended to the world.

To be in Union requires Transparency, surrender, non-judgment and Love. Until that state of being is perfected, we practice. Sacred Union is a spiritual practice. Like any discipline it requires attention and commitment to return to the practice each time you catch yourself in ego-reactivity. The quality of your Union will depend upon your willingness to return to Unconditional Love. Self-Ascension is a spiral[14] of ever-refining love.

We all have a *self* that we identify with. This self is usually our personality and includes our bodily appearance. Over time we learn to look beyond personality and physicality. The spiritual practice of relationship uses the partnership to support an expansion of consciousness. This results is an expansion of Love, an expansion of Peace, and an expansion of Joy. Peace, Love and Joy are the qualities of the Self-Ascended state; of soul consciousness.

To be ever more authentic with each other requires Transparency. It also requires that you consciously work to perfect the Union by being in agreement. I am not referring to intellectual differences; I am referring to energetic agreement. Energetic agreement refers to those activities, people, and objects that influence your felt experience. Rather than seek to negotiate differences, it is better to first seek to expand what you do agree on. By increasing commonalities, you enhance the Union.

Never allow something into your shared life that does not feel good for both of you. For example, do not buy a piece of furniture that you both do not enjoy. More importantly, do not allow people into your experience that you both are not aligned with. Whenever you are together, be sure to tune in with your body and see if you are holding tension or discomfort. That is your clue. Pay attention, for you are not able to be fully present due to an inner resistance of some sort. It is your job to bring that resistance to consciousness through transparency.

If you both are not feeling relaxed or joyful around an individual then do not spend relationship time with that person. It may be that you will need to bring your feelings to the Union and explore them together. You do not have to be at peace with everyone, with every situation. Start by knowing what brings you Joy and what does not. Over time, and with ongoing sharing, love, and deepening of the Union, you will discover that experiences become easier to enjoy.

[14]See Self-Ascension Chakra Portrait in Appendix

Healing will be triggered by the presence of certain individuals or situations. However, until that healing is accomplished do not ask one of the partners to compromise. Compromise is death. It is like burying someone alive; with each compromise one loses a bit of vitality and loses touch with their true feelings and life force. Far better to avoid the compromise situations and simply do the things and be with the people you both enjoy. No compromises! No have-to! Do what fulfills you! Step-by-step you will build a more fulfilling relationship. Step-by-step you will deepen trust and intimacy. Step-by-step the Union will cultivate a portal for Self-Ascension. This is the path of the *Yumi* soul.

What is the *Yumi* soul? It's a fun word that Kira offered to describe the union of *You* and *Me*. Once the commitment is made to be in Union, to be Transparent and energetically aligned, then you no longer exist as a separate entity. You become unified with your partner. If you are one of the two billion people on the planet that is a member of our soul group, then this Union is serious business. Your souls truly become one. You will start knowing the thoughts of each other.

What was your personal identity becomes an aspect of the unified soul. I am the male aspect; Kira Raa is the female aspect. We still have a life of our own, but that individual life exists in the context of the Union, the Yumi soul.

The only real pain is separation from my partner. I am not referring to physical separation. I have learned that when I am energetically disconnected from Kira I feel pain. If I slip into judgment or hurt, I have collapsed into my ego. This creates a field of separation between my Beloved and myself that we both feel. It essentially doubles the pain. I experience the pain of my own ego defenses plus the pain of separation from the Beloved. The ego defenses that cause separation are the very structures that need love and healing. So the Union becomes both the catalyst and the cure for self-defeating thoughts and feelings. It is a beautiful healing synergy.

No, it is not easy to be Transparent. Yet it becomes easy. Once you have tasted the Peace and Love of the Sacred Union you will not be satisfied with anything less. Once you have allowed the Union to heal your fears, why would you choose autonomy? Once you know Joy, why would you go back to a life of secrets, pain and compromise?

Sacred Union is true marriage and the blending of energies of the individuals into a unified soul. I am Sri Ram Kaa. My beloved is Kira Raa. We have become the Sri Ram Kaa Kira Raa. We are now complete.

I thank God for my bride, my Beloved partner, and my other half. I thank God for my consciousness. I thank God for this mission, and the opportunity to serve the awakening of our planet. May we all come to know the truth of our Being.

Appendix

Soul Nourishment Program

If you decide to embark on the soul nourishment program, it is imperative you sincerely embrace *all* of its components. The program is not designed to be a diet, it is meant to create an energetic synergism in your vessel to enhance Authenticity and increase your energy vibration. This is an amazing frequency that opens your door to the Peace, Love, and Joy of the Self-Ascension process. We have both experienced enhanced vitality, not just from the foods we ingest, but from the synergy of all the loving practices.

Some of the benefits we have experienced are reversed aging, enhanced energy, clarity, and physical balance (weight loss). Sri Ram Kaa experienced a reversal of osteoarthritis symptoms, and the benefits continue to accrue. Appreciating every day with both morning and evening Self-Ascension practices has supported rapid results.

You do not have to become a vegetarian overnight. It is far easier to add something into your diet than it is to take away what you are used to. So if you are a "meat and potatoes" kind of person, be gentle with yourself. Start by adding generous servings of vegetables to your diet. Enjoy a big salad at lunchtime. Discard beef but keep chicken and fish in your diet for a few weeks. Eliminate milk products. Begin adding in tofu and as you acquire a taste for soy protein, then discard the chicken. Give yourself time for your pallet to adjust. Take a month or more to transition.

We came by our results honestly. We experienced some periods of detoxification that were uncomfortable. And we have both justified things we should not have eaten. It was really powerful to rationalize eating something that does not serve, and then discover first-hand how uncomfortable the body felt afterwards. The purer we become, the easier it is to simply know what is healthy and what is not healthy to put into our vessels. At a certain point along the way, inappropriate food simply tastes heavy or toxic in the mouth. One bite and you know.

Daily Nourishment Components:

Kiel provided us with two guidelines regarding our daily consumption of nourishment (food):

Nothing of the cow.
Nothing from a can.

When we first began this program we both were still eating limited fish. To provide us with an adjustment time, Kiel suggested three weeks to wean ourselves from the fish and adapt to other forms of protein. Kiel also made clear not to eat any meat, and the term, "nothing of the cow," specifically pointed to the need to eliminate dairy[15].

Provide your system with plenty of fresh, pure water. After all, water is a great conduit of electricity and your energy will respond favorably to the extra boost. If you need to put some fresh lemon in your water, this is fine.

Include, daily, some form of leafy green vegetable in your food. Including greens at two meals a day is optimal. Make sure to include a vegetable protein with at least one meal. We find soy products wonderful, and there are lots of amazingly tasty new vegan foods available.

Fruits and grains should be part of your daily routine. Starting the day with fresh fruit, oatmeal, and whole grain cereal are also excellent. If you take the time to cook the oatmeal in soymilk and sweeten it with maple syrup you might just surprise yourself.

Every thirty days Kiel suggests a cleansing of the vessel. For these two days it is liquids only. This means juices, smoothies and soups. We still drink our water on these two days and we have actually come to look forward to how creative we can be. We have started making wonderful soups, and will often make a blend of a squash based soup with a green soup. We have had fun making the recipes and enjoying how creative these two days can be.

Follow the two-day liquid cleanse with a day of just vegetables and fruit before reintroducing grain and protein into the diet.

Daily exercise

After being on the soul nourishment program for about three weeks, Kiel added exercise of the physical body to the program. He

---

[15]Note: It was compatible with the rising vibration to eat goat cheese. If you are currently eating meat or fish, we would suggest the same three week period to wean off.

was loving and clear that this was a meditative process, and should be thought of as such.

During this time, it is of benefit to focus on the love that you are and to call in the energy of the Peace, Love and Joy from the universe. This is a time of simple gratitude for your vessel as a remembrance that the vessel serves you and that you are able to say *thank you* by moving it.

To keep it simple, there were only two forms of meditative exercise that Kiel suggested, and those were gentle yoga and walking. He also made it clear that even if we only invested 5 minutes a day, the results would be positive. Certainly one can do more, but 5 to 10 minutes twice a day was quite easy to fit in to our schedule. The goal was to stretch and move the body while holding a prayerful attitude. This provided harmony between body and soul.

He was right. Each time we finish our walking or yoga, there is an immense charge in the energy system. It is better than a nap, and it feels wonderful to treat yourself to a fresh made carrot juice afterwards.

Evening Soul Nourishment

It is important to incorporate the evening practice of gratitude prior to sleeping. As your vibrational level increases, your level of gratitude will increase also. Give it a voice.

As you lay down to sleep at night, simply allow your face to smile as you close your eyes and breathe. Call to your memory everything of the day for which you are grateful. Include your vessel which has so lovingly supported you during the day. Your vessel has given you the gift of life on this planet. Relax and give gratitude to yourself for all the accomplishments of the day, knowing that all is as it should be. Whatever you accomplished was right and perfect.

Would you like to be one of those people who sees that the cup is half full instead of half empty? Then gratitude is your primary Self-Ascension practice! The universe is an abundant place. Throughout the day, allow yourself to verbally share your gratitude with others. Rather than refrain from stating appreciation, have fun by seeing how much you are truly grateful for! State it out loud. You will be amazed at how much better "the Flow" becomes when you are grateful for what comes your way. The energy infusion from the gift of gratitude is enormous. An attitude of gratitude also expands your heart and nourishes the people who enter your space.

Your first few days of the entire soul nourishment program could be challenging, depending upon your prior habits. Know that you have a choice. You are in charge of your ego. You are in charge of your body. Start implementing changes by first summoning the energy of Joy and then choosing a part of the soul-nourishment program to implement. Once you start connecting with your authenticity, and as your energy vibrational level increases, it will become effortless. The Peace, Love and Joy will sustain you.

Self-Ascension Chakra Portrait

The Self-Ascension chakra portrait represents the vibrational shift that occurs as you surrender to the Peace, Love and Joy of Self-Ascension. This portrait was divinely provided to Kira during a time of deep meditation.

The star (two triangles overlapping each other), represents the integration of the masculine and feminine energy. The golden portal is the container that holds the space for Self-Ascension. As the physical body and the soul grow closer in the embrace of Authenticity, the chakras begin to vibrate at a new level of energy. Each of the traditional chakra points is shown in its Ascended state. The lotus chakra at the top is referred to commonly as the eighth chakra. The red chakra at the bottom is frequently known as the root, or first chakra.

Kiel has recommended that we spend 5 minutes a day, simply focused upon the portrait. Breathing into the space of allowing ourselves to open to the energy and feel the bliss of the golden portal.

Simply start by taking in the portrait as a whole. Is there a point that is particularly calling you? If so, go there. You may also wish to begin by following the golden portal, feeling the surging energy flow.

After you have relaxed into the vibration of the portrait allow yourself to first focus your attention on the root or red chakra. Visualize this energy moving into you, allow Peace, Love and Joy to enter into your energy center.

Continue the process of visualizing energy as you move up through all of the chakra centers. Breathing in a "circular" fashion also greatly enhances the experience of the energy.

To breathe in this fashion, simply breathe in deeply through your nose, then swirl the breath through your entire body, deeply exhale the breath. As soon as the breath has released, immediately take in your next inhalation.

To enhance this experience you may wish to use a larger, full-color rendering of the Chakra Portrait. Please visit our web site, www.SelfAscension.com, or you can order a color poster by mail.

Self-Ascension Chakra Portrait

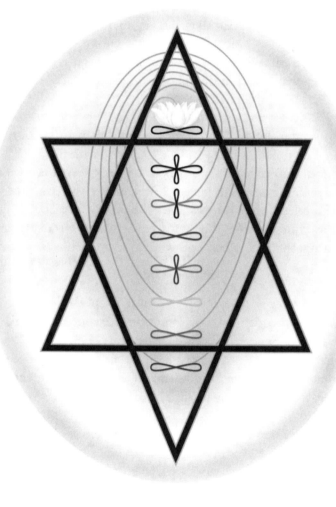

Self-Ascension Practices

Aura Stretching:

Your aura is simply an energy field that surrounds the body, the existence of which has been proven by many varied scientific methods. It is not important that you are able to see your aura or that you are aware of its colors. What is paramount is that you allow yourself to become aware of how your aura *feels*. It is a subtle energy vibration that can be a welcome friend of protection when it is recognized and strengthened properly.

Kiel provided us with this exercise as a means to further strengthen our individual aura, along with the connection to the divine. He recommends that you start each day with this exercise. You can even do it before leaving your bed. Kiel suggests that you can do the aura stretching often. It offers refreshment and essential vitality whenever unpleasant emotions are present. It is also effective to simply allow yourself an "infusion of light" which is most pleasurable and peaceful, especially when you wish to calm, center and balance.

Sit comfortably and begin by breathing deeply. Allow your eyes to close gently as you center your attention on your aura. Take a few moments to experience the boundary of your energy field.

Familiar now with the outer edge of your aura, send energy to stretch your aura out as far as you can so that it can connect with the divine energy of the universe. Simply stretch your aura out in front, in back, below you and above you. Send it in all directions. Release any pre-conceived judgments about time and space and relax into the stretching.

At some point you will notice a tingle or a sense of vitality; allow the energy cosmos to re-energize your aura. Take a moment to experience this state of oneness. When you are ready, allow your newly re-energized aura to return to its normal state, near your body. Continue deep breathing, slowly open your eyes, and enjoy!

The Star Practice

The Star Exercise will activate much Authenticity.

The golden star in the third eye joins all of the chakras, generates peace, and creates love. If you bring your attention to this area whenever you are feeling any type of conflict, competition or pain, it will balance your energy and return you to Authenticity.

Responding in anger is merely one of the ego's self-defense mechanisms. As anger is released and projected, it actually damages the psyche. This psyche damage will prevent your vibrational level from the energetic tuning that is needed to embrace the energy shift for Self-Ascension.

The alternative to anger, is to reside in a state of love. By remaining peaceful, we do not engage the ego. By using the Star Practice often, you are creating the habit of peace. The more you are able to call in your own Peace, Love and Joy, the simpler it becomes to maintain your authenticity.

❦

(The instructions given for this exercise include a partner. Your partner should sit opposite you, and your knees should be touching your partners knees. If you do not have a partner to practice, simply sit in front of a mirror and enjoy the experience.)

With your eyes open and your hands together in prayer position, relax and focus your gaze on the 3rd eye (center of forehead) of your partner. Your hands are in front of your heart chakra with your thumbs touching the center of your chest, and your fingers pointed outward.

Start by imagining a glowing beautiful star on your forehead. As you feel into your star, allow yourself to send the brilliant loving energy into the star of the other person.

As you are radiating this brilliant energy allow the words "I love you, I know you, I honor your divinity," to float on your thoughts.

Your loving energy will open your partner's third eye and help them to remember their own Authenticity. This exercise is a focusing of love toward the other, and especially helpful if you are in an uncomfortable situation. You can do the Star Practice silently whenever you find yourself confronting a challenging person or situation.

The Star Practice has other applications as well. It is a centering exercise that is quick and beneficial. When you practice this alone, it also provides grounding in your Authenticity and promotes a habit of peaceful, loving feelings.

This can also be done with an animal as a practice partner, or simply to engage the healing energy with a loved companion.

An expanded form of the exercise is to bless the planet. It is a simple variation to do this. Relax and allow your third eye to merge with the planetary energies as you visualize them. Exhale deeply and often during the planetary exercise.

Telepathy Exercise

This is an advanced exercise, and synergistic with the practice of Transparent Communication. To embrace this energy, it is important to prepare the vessel with the soul nourishment program. Eating eggs, for example, inhibits telepathy. The intent of the exercise is to increase trust and love between couples, and to create a bond of love through a deeper integration of the Self-Ascension steps.

(This exercise requires a partner.)

Begin by sitting back to back with your partner. If you can, it is preferable to sit on the floor with the shoes off. Do some deep breathing together, allowing your breathing to become in sync with one another. Be open to sharing all thoughts during the exercise.

Continue to align your spines and breathing until you feel as one.

The Receiver is the first to speak. There are three minutes of "sending" the thoughts before the Receiver starts to speak them back to the Sender. During the three minutes the Sender should be focused only on the thought being sent. The Receiver should focus on trusting what they are hearing.

When you first begin, you often miss the reception because it happens so fast that you just do not hear it. As you practice the exercise more, develop greater trust for the very first thought you receive; you will find that this is usually the sent message.

When the three minutes has ended, and after the Receiver shares what they hear or sense, it is beneficial to have a dialogue about the experience. It is important to include sharing all fears, emotions, feelings about the exercise with each other.

Take a short break and stretch. Then come back together, re-energize and synchronize the breath as you align your spines and begin the process again. Now the other partner is the Receiver for three minutes of silence before sharing.

Kiel suggested these practice phrases for the Sender to hold in their thoughts:

I love you.

I trust you.

There is only Joy.

Cycle through the complete telepathy exercise three times in a session, with each partner being both Sender and Receiver three times.

After practicing this exercise for a few weeks with your partner, you will discover there is no Sender, no Receiver, only One!

Telepathy transmission follows complete surrender. Doubt blocks the transmission. Fear of losing your mind blocks transmission. Actually, it *is* losing the mind without connection with the bliss that is the problem. Talking is heavy. Telepathy is blissful.

Transparent Communication on a daily and committed basis is important preparation. By building the bonds of trust inside the union, it helps to eliminate fear and supports Unconditional Love and surrender.

Advanced Self-Ascension Practice

The Rods of the Pharaohs

By taking a careful look at the photographs of the statues of Egyptian Pharaohs and Priests, you will notice them holding small cylindrical objects in their hands.

Recently recovered documents from a Mystery School indicate that these rods were used for healing, expansion of consciousness, balancing of vital energy, and Ascension. The rods were replicated and have been studied in Russia since 1994.

The Russian studies are quite thorough. They have been conducted with medical doctors, physicists, psychologists, Kirlian photography experts, and other researchers investigating the effects of these Rods on human beings. They have documented many health benefits. You will find more information on the Rods at www.EgyptianHealingRods.com

The Rods of the Pharaohs are indeed a wonderful gift that has been rediscovered. Kira Raa and I have worked with these Rods extensively. We can offer that they do, in fact, offer heightened connectivity for couples. They open the chakras, enhance meditation, and seem to have an overall healing effect on the bio field. They are indeed Ascension technology and greatly assist the development of energy awareness.

Here is what the Russian manufacturer has to say about the Rods:

"As a result of the rods influence on a human organism, the general energetic level increases. The bio-energy redistributes itself between the organs and systems more harmonically, and pathological misbalance is removed. Protective functions are activated and the organism is shifted to a state where it is much easier for it to cope with any problems. Thus, the people suffering from different diseases can consider the Rods as their powerful helper in their struggle for health. Besides, the Rods help with insomnia, headaches, hypertension, stresses, and thus may help avoid using chemical remedies."

The Rods are not required for Self-Ascension; however, they do accelerate progress. There are several types of Rods available. We recommend the "Rods-CrystalStar™" to accelerate your Self-Ascension work. This Rod set is the most powerful. If you have health problems or are in a weakened state then you should begin with the gentler "Rods-Quartz." This practice can be included as part of your daily devotional activity. It is also an effective stress reducer and will help balance the energy between the partners. Whether used individually or as a couple, the Egyptian Healing Rods stimulate energetic balance thus making it easier to connect consciously with your Soul's energy.

Rods Exercise:

This practice can be effective individually or by sharing a set of Egyptian Healing Rods with a partner. It is optimal to do this meditation outside, barefoot, and facing the sun. However, if it is windy or if there is inclement weather then indoor practice is acceptable.

Stand facing the direction of the sun. (Note: In the evening face west, at night face north.) Take a few moments to center yourself and then join hands. The male partner offers his right hand to the female's left hand. You'll share one set of Rods by holding the Rods in the free hands. The female should take the Sun Rod (copper rod) in her right hand; the male should take the Moon Rod (zinc rod) in his left hand.

a) The Sun (copper) Rod must be held in the right hand only, and the Moon (zinc) Rod—in the left hand, never vice versa.

b) Squeeze the Rods in your hands tightly for approximately 1 minute to activate the connection. Then relax your grip to a comfortable level and straighten the arms alongside the body. Facing the sun, advance your left leg a half-step.

c) Release your thoughts or concentrate them on the Sun, which gives light and life to every living creature. Smile with happiness, relax your muscles, lower the shoulders, relax your facial muscles, and then keep the sense of smiling inside yourself.

d) Begin to pace your breathing so that the inhalation is balanced with the exhalation. Inhale to the silent count of 7, hold for 1 count, and then exhale to the count of 7, hold for 1 count and continue. Note: if a 7 count doesn't feel comfortable then adjust your count to a pace that is comfortable for you, the key is to balance the inhalation with the exhalation.

e) After you have created a rhythm, just relax into your Being-ness. *Optional: If your mind wanders then bring it back to the breath. Imagine on the in-breath that you are inhaling God's love and on the out-breath you are sending love to all Beings.*

f) The exercise should be done for a minimum of seven minutes and not longer than 18 minutes.

g) After you release the Rods you might enjoy lying down and relaxing. This promotes a deeper energetic conditioning and health-improving effect from the Rod exercise.

The Russian research indicates that energy flows between the couple. The energy will flow from the stronger person to weaker, without any loss to the stronger one. This results in an energetic balance.

Couples who are energetically harmonized will find it easier to address relationship challenges and the stress that confronts us in a modern society.

Portals of Love
the story of the cover painting
By Victoria Kwasinski

It is a great honor and privilege to be a part of this divine experience. I believe we are all being called to honor our authenticity and transcend to a new consciousness. My path is the gift of my passion; Art. I am called to paint images of healing for all life, and life is love, and love is God.

I have weathered many tumultuous relationships along the journey of my path. I have worked on spiritual growth for many years. Seeking healing and union with God.

Through a good friend of Sri Ram Kaa and Kira Raa, I was an invited guest at their wedding. This was the first time we met. I was guided to bring as a gift, a print of a painting I had completed five years ago, depicting angels uniting the globe. Angels have a powerful place in my life, and little did I know the significance of presenting this divinely guided gift.

My heart was so touched at the marriage ceremony! There was a feeling of love that radiated out to all of us who where there. The words Sri Ram Kaa and Kira Raa exchanged brought tears of joy to my eyes. The experience was divine. I now know that I was guided to be there.

In the early hours of the morning following the wedding, I had a dream that was both powerful and beautiful. I rarely remember my dreams, and am usually guided by visions in an awakened or meditative state. This dream would not leave me. I spent several hours when I awoke drawing and journaling about the dream.

The message of the vision and the drawing became clear and revealed itself as the healing of our relationships. Leaving the shadow side, old patterns, and belief systems that cause the splintering in humanity. Crossing barriers and walls of the ego to the new paradigm, where we are led through portals of love. Learning to accept, embrace, and honor the divine that is within each of us as we enter into relationship. Through this transcendence, we experience unconditional love and discover the true purpose of relationship is the union of souls into oneness.

I put the sketch away with the intention of painting it at some future time. A few weeks later, Kira Raa called to thank me for the angel print. She asked if I would be interested in doing some work for their new book.

On the meeting day, while preparing my typical portfolio package, I was guided to bring along the journal that contained the drawing from my dream. I felt a connection with Sri Ram Kaa and Kira Raa, and the journal drawing was the last thing I showed them. Instantaneously we all knew it was to be the cover for this book.

Many other small miracles occurred in the color version of the painting you see on the cover. I am delighted that the message from my heart and the gift of my Art is being used to send the message of love and light. I hope the image inspires you to seek and find the joy of oneness.

Thank you Sri Ram Kaa and Kira Raa for sharing your story and your love; and for honoring me in allowing to share mine.

Victoria Kwasinski is a freelance Fine Artist, Illustrator, and Instructor. The purpose of her journey and path is to bring joy to others through the gift of her Art. She can be contacted through the website she shares with other artists of similar artistic intentions: www.prisma4.com.